Pr ...
Grace un ...

Replete with timely illustrations and grace-filled applications, this is a one-stop resource for anyone looking to preach, teach, or study how Jesus addressed and conquered unspeakable strain and stress. Chris Kennedy begins with a multi-chapter introduction that focuses on the twin themes of his book—God's grace and life's pressure points. He then digs deeply into Christ's seven last words from the cross, showing how they address our need for divine grace, especially when our hearts break into a million pieces.

—Rev. Dr. Reed Lessing,
PROFESSOR OF THEOLOGY AND MINISTRY AND
DIRECTOR OF THE CENTER FOR BIBLICAL STUDIES,
CONCORDIA UNIVERSITY ST. PAUL

For anyone experiencing the stresses of life, *Grace under Pressure* provides a way forward in the strength of the Lord. In this book, Dr. Christopher Kennedy first identifies the pressures and tempta-tions people often feel today. He then shares a message of hope from the One who gives ultimate grace when facing life's greatest pressures. In a series of Christ-centered Lenten messages, first enjoyed by his congregation, this pastor shares with his readers the comforting mes-sage of Jesus' ministry centered on His cross and empty tomb. It is a powerful message of hope and strength born of grace under pressure!

—Rev. Dr. W. Mart Thompson,
ASSOCIATE PROFESSOR OF PRACTICAL THEOLOGY,
CONCORDIA SEMINARY, ST. LOUIS

An unfaithful response to stress is easy and comes naturally. Pastor Kennedy offers real, practical guidance for a "new creation" response to life's many stress-inducing situations: the cross of Jesus! In the Lord's words from the cross, Pastor Kennedy helps baptized children of God find grace and strength for a Gospel-driven way to deal with many of our daily challenges. There's guidance here for all who want to exhibit less "me" and more Jesus in the words and deeds of their daily Christian walk.

—Rev. Dr. Darrell Zimmerman, EXECUTIVE DIRECTOR OF GRACE PLACE
WELLNESS MINISTRIES, LUTHERAN CHURCH EXTENSION FUND

Our ungracious world desperately needs the fullness of God's grace. Chris Kennedy describes richly the many facets of the gift of grace. Grace is God's presence with us in the wildest storm. God's grace is found especially in the darkness of Good Friday through the seven words of Jesus that day. On the cross, true grace was spoken with words of forgiveness for sinners, hope for a dying man, and the trust of a Son being caught by a loving Father.

—Dr. Daniel Paavola,
professor, Concordia University Wisconsin

Grace under Pressure takes the reader into the words and life of Jesus—as He walked the path for us—and walks with us! In an easy-to-digest format, each chapter follows Jesus to the cross, with thoughtful discussion and study questions at the end. This is ideal for a personal or group study. Chris has captured the struggle every reader has with life's stresses, and he offers a Gospel-oriented assurance of Jesus' presence in the midst of that stress!

—Rev. James Otte, MDiv, MEd, LPC,
associate pastor, Messiah Lutheran Church,
Texas District director of congregation and worker care

I love it when an author puts forward his or her perspectives, offers help for discussion, and then encourages those discussions. Such conversations make for growth for all the followers of Jesus. Chris Kennedy does that with this book. There are some points that Kennedy makes about stress management that I would like to challenge. That is good. That is the point of the book. At the foot of the cross and in the power of the empty tomb, let's talk openly about life issues. This book is ideal for group discussion and, if someone would invite me, I'd work to attend.

—Rev. Dr. Bruce M. Hartung,
emeritus professor of practical theology,
Concordia Seminary, St. Louis;
author of *Holding Up the Prophet's Hand* and
Building Up the Body of Christ

GRACE UNDER PRESSURE

Responding Faithfully to Stress

CHRISTOPHER M. KENNEDY

With a Foreword by
Paul L. Maier, PhD

CONCORDIA PUBLISHING HOUSE · SAINT LOUIS

Published by Concordia Publishing House
3558 S. Jefferson Avenue, St. Louis, MO 63118-3968
1-800-325-3040 • cph.org

See p. 167 for further acknowledgments.

Cover image © Shutterstock.com

Manufactured in the United States of America

1 2 3 4 5 6 7 8 9 10   31 30 29 28 27 26 25 24 23 22

This book is dedicated with love to my son Ethan. Ethan, you have a heart of gold. You are one of the kindest, most thoughtful people I've ever met. I'm so proud of the person God has made you to be. Your kindness will be tested by stressful situations and challenges. With God's help, you will be up to the task. I pray for God to fill you with His Spirit so that you may show the grace of Jesus in good times and hard times. Your mom and I love you and are here to support you always.

Contents

FOREWORD

Many books have titles that only vaguely suggest their contents. This is not one of them. Christopher Kennedy has written a book featuring Jesus' last statements on the Good Friday cross that could not have been better presented than *Grace under Pressure*. None better, because no better example of grace or pressure is possible. Grace covers the generous provenance of God and refers to the ultimate gifts of forgiveness and eternal life to believers, and pressure involves the horrendous circumstances of Jesus' crucifixion. Despite pressure from atoning for the incalculable mass of human sin since creation, our Lord testified to the grace of God to all humanity in His suffering and death: the most righteous individual who ever lived suffering the worst penalties conceivable—grace under pressure indeed!

In these pages, Kennedy, a Christian pastor in San Antonio, Texas, provides well-crafted material for a Lenten series of sermons, which indeed they were in his own congregation, and which prompted this book. It could also serve as a study for a class of adults, or near adults, since he has included a thought-provoking set of questions at the end of each chapter that will stimulate discussion.

The author shows his skills as a first-class homiletician. In these meditations, which are extremely appropriate as to doctrine and application in reporting on Jesus that fateful day, Kennedy regularly employs Scripture in support of his theological views without "stretching" any of his insights.

His book opens by discussing why the world needs God's grace today and one major cause of modern problems: stress. Very likely, the planet has witnessed more stress due to the demands of the accelerated existence we have today, politically, economically, socially, and intellectually, which have robbed us of happiness and peace of mind. No one can quarrel with this statement as they sigh, "Where are the wonderful days of yesteryear?" On checking it out, however, one finds that sin is largely responsible for muddying the waters, in previous generations as well as now. Christ is the answer to our crying need for God's grace and effective spiritual solutions.

The author provides sparkling illustrations based on Scripture and other appropriate sources: David and Solomon, for example, who lived gracefully until they succumbed to pressure and stresses that they themselves caused and ended their days gracelessly. Other historical figures up to the present day are also mentioned, such as the author himself or Dr. Robert Cade, a Lutheran and the inventor of Gatorade, in the chapter in which Jesus says, "I thirst."

This book also ripples with brilliant illustrations of how this has worked in this pastor's professional life and can work well also for others, clergy or laity. These are just a few examples from this well-written book in which there is not a dull line.

I found myself surprisingly in need of Kennedy's suggestions while preparing for my own latest book on Jesus. During my dictation to my secretary, too much stress often led me to raise my voice whenever she wanted a sentence repeated. And I could not recall the *perfect way* I had presented it the first time (only then feeling like a worm for raising my voice rather than demonstrating Christian patience as I should have done). In this regard, I warmly endorse this book for all Christian leaders who may have had similar problems in failing to celebrate God's grace as Jesus did, the model for us all.

PAUL L. MAIER, PHD
PROFESSOR EMERITUS OF ANCIENT HISTORY,
WESTERN MICHIGAN UNIVERSITY

Author of Josephus: The Essential Writings,
The Genuine Jesus: Fresh Evidence from History and
Archaeology, *and* A Skeleton in God's Closet

PREFACE

In 1 Corinthians 11:1, the apostle Paul wrote, "Be imitators of me, as I am of Christ."

If you want to respond gracefully to the pressures of life, look to the cross. You'll find no greater exhibition of love while under intense strain than Jesus. His conduct on the cross is the defining moment of grace in all of history.

We all face pressures. Appropriate levels of stress are necessary and healthy. Excessive stress, however, is more than God designed us to handle. When we're stretched beyond our capacity, we're overloading the system our Creator engineered. The purpose of this book is to help you live more gracefully when faced with *excessive stress*. The fuel for graceful living is God's love that "has been poured into our hearts through the Holy Spirit" (Romans 5:5).

The genesis of this book was a Lenten sermon series. On Ash Wednesday, five Sundays in Lent, and Good Friday, I preached on the seven words of Jesus from the cross. The series resonated with my congregation, and I hope the messages will encourage you too.

This book is divided into two parts. Part 1 sets up the seven last statements by exploring themes of grace and stress in our world today, in the Bible, and in Jesus' life. Part 1 ends by providing context for what Jesus experienced on the cross. Part 2 is a study of the seven last statements, highlighting Jesus' graceful words and actions.

You may be suffering under excessive stress right now. I pray this book will help you navigate your challenges in a God-honoring way.

"Grace was given to each one of us according to the measure of Christ's gift" (Ephesians 4:7). God grant you a full measure of His gift of grace today and always.

CHRISTOPHER M. KENNEDY
SAN ANTONIO, TEXAS
DECEMBER 2020

PART 1

The Necessity of Grace

We wouldn't need to be graceful if life were easy. But life isn't easy. Stress is an inescapable reality. Sometimes we feel pushed to the limit by our circumstances. Pressure was just as unavoidable for people in the Bible, even for Jesus Himself. His earthly ministry was filled with demands, opposition, and situations that tested His resolve. The cross was the culmination of His pressure-packed ministry.

But He said to me, "My grace is sufficient for you, for My power is made perfect in weakness." Therefore I will boast all the more gladly of my weaknesses, so that the power of Christ may rest upon me. For the sake of Christ, then, I am content with weaknesses, insults, hardships, persecutions, and calamities. For when I am weak, then I am strong.

2 CORINTHIANS 12:9–10

CHAPTER 1

LIVING GRACEFULLY

I saw the crash coming. The crushing of metal was painful to witness. The human reaction afterward was hard to watch too.

At their own peril, cars cross the intersection of Huebner and Fredericksburg Roads in San Antonio. For the second time in months, I witnessed an accident at the intersection. Two cars, coming from opposite directions, tried to occupy the same space at the same moment, a physical impossibility. The cars collided.

One woman emerged from her car looking dazed. Her body shook. Her face was ghostly white.

The other driver stormed out of her car like a rocket. Her face was tomato red. She didn't ask the other driver if she was all right. She didn't say, "It's okay. It was an accident. Things happen."

No, she stomped up to the driver and exploded in a tirade of expletives. I've forgotten most of her words, but I do remember one exclamation: "That car was my life!"

I've previously encountered people after auto accidents. Usually they're rattled, shaken, disoriented. I'd never seen a person go into attack mode like that in the immediate aftermath of an accident.

Let's give the woman the benefit of the doubt. Perhaps she was already having a bad day and was one more catastrophe away from blowing up. Maybe she had depleted her entire life savings to purchase the car. Maybe she'd owned the car for most of her adult life, and it was her most cherished possession. It's possible she grew up in a household where screaming was the norm for handling conflict.

I don't know her story. All I know is that she responded to a stressful situation loudly and aggressively.

I'm in no position to judge her. I've responded to situations poorly myself. Chief of sinners—that's me.

Like me, you've probably had your share of ungraceful moments. You've also probably observed others react in ways that were uncomfortable to watch. *Ungraceful* is hard to define with words. But you know it when you see it.

Ungraceful behavior is losing your cool and screaming at your children.

Ungraceful behavior is belittling your spouse.

Ungraceful behavior is losing self-control over your eating, drinking, or spending.

Ungraceful behavior is road rage.

Ungraceful behavior is venting over social media.

Ungraceful behavior is political debaters verbally assaulting one another with low blows.

Ungraceful behavior is blaming others.

Ungraceful behavior is "woe is me" self-pity.

You get the picture. No doubt, you can add to the list. Ungraceful behavior pervades our society and often our own homes.

The Root of Ungracefulness

Where do our ungraceful reactions come from?

When we're under pressure, two factors collide: our sinful nature and difficult circumstances. We are broken people living in a broken world. The combination can be devastating.

Feeling stress is not a sin. Feelings aren't sins. God created us as emotional beings. How we respond to feelings can be sinful.

When we react to stress with pettiness, we're not honoring God. When we explode in anger, we're not treating others as God desires. In those moments, rather than the Holy Spirit having His way, our sinful nature dictates our behaviors.

The Bible traces our sinful nature to the dawn of history. When Adam and Eve rebelled against God in the Garden of Eden, sin invaded the human race: "Sin came into the world through one man" (Romans 5:12). Sin became a part of our DNA, transmitted through every generation. We're contaminated even before we're born, as it says in Psalm 51:5: "I was brought forth in iniquity, and in sin did my mother conceive me." Scripture describes us as "children of wrath" (Ephesians 2:3) and says that "everyone who practices sin is a slave to sin" (John 8:34).

Our sinful nature means we're inclined toward wrongdoing. We're predisposed to lose our cool, blow up, and make a mess of things. We're volatile beings. We're storms brewing. The potential for sinful actions is always there. An alignment of wrong conditions stirs up the storm within. The result can be minimal damage or devastating destruction.

That's how it works. Circumstances press upon our sinful nature and push us over the edge. We express God-given feelings in ungodly ways. Under pressure, we have a hard time containing our discomfort. Others bear the brunt of our reactivity.

With God's Help

How do we break the cycle of ungraceful words and actions? I aspire to be a more graceful person, and you probably do too.

One of the most encouraging notes I've ever received was attached to a birthday present a few years ago. The note said, in part, "I know this is a tough season, and I admire the grace, poise, and leadership you continue to show. May God continue to give you the wisdom and guidance to shepherd His people."

Those three words meant the world to me: *grace*, *poise*, and *leadership*. I keep the note in my desk as a reminder of those ideals. At the time the note was given to me, I didn't feel like the words applied. But knowing that someone else saw those qualities in me instilled confidence, and it cultivated gratitude in my heart. The gratitude was partly toward my friend for such a generous attribution. The bulk of the gratitude, however, was toward God.

During that tough season, whatever grace, poise, and leadership I showed was to God's credit alone. None of us are at our best under stress. Left to our own devices under pressure, we're more likely to exhibit the characteristics of ungraceful living. With God's help, we can respond differently. We can be graceful people.

I want to emphasize that point: *with God's help*. On our own, we struggle to resist our impulses. We lose our composure and become overly reactive. Left to ourselves, we inflict pain on others and ourselves.

By faith in Jesus, we have help. Jesus promised His followers, "I will ask the Father, and He will give you another Helper, to be with you forever" (John 14:16). The Helper, whom Jesus identifies as "the Spirit of truth" (v. 17), brings us to faith and enables us to live holy lives. Even when we're under stress, the Holy Spirit is active in us and can produce godliness.

Romans 8 teaches us about life in the Spirit. Believers "walk not according to the flesh but according to the Spirit" (v. 4). Walking according to the Spirit has a tangible effect on how we live. Galatians 5:22–23 lists the fruit of the Spirit, the by-product of Jesus dwelling in your heart by faith: "But the fruit of the Spirit is love, joy, peace, patience, kindness, goodness, faithfulness, gentleness, self-control."

The items in that list are exactly what we need! With God's help, we can live gracefully, even when trials and troubles press down on us.

God's Grace and Our Grace

Grace is one of the most wonderful words in the English language and one of the most beautiful concepts in the Bible. "By grace you have been saved through faith" (Ephesians 2:8). It doesn't get any better than that!

The overwhelming majority of references to *grace* in the Bible, particularly in the New Testament, refer to God's grace, the source of our salvation. Some will distinguish between different kinds of grace, in an effort to explore the magnitude of God's love—its "breadth and length and height and depth" (Ephesians 3:18). Consider these possible dimensions of grace:

- ◆ Common grace, the gifts God gives to all people as Creator; "He makes His sun rise on the evil and on the good, and sends rain on the just and on the unjust" (Matthew 5:45).

- ◆ Saving grace, God's gift of forgiveness and eternal life through Jesus.

- ◆ Sanctifying grace, the Holy Spirit's work in us to produce spiritual fruit and godly living.

- ◆ Sustaining grace, the strength God provides us to withstand trials: "My grace is sufficient for you, for My power is made perfect in weakness" (2 Corinthians 12:9).

Thinking in these categories, the grace we exhibit under pressure could be considered sanctifying grace or sustaining grace. In the midst of trials, God sustains us and empowers us to bear spiritual fruit, even under adverse conditions. As our Creator, Savior, and Helper, God is the source of all grace. Empowered by His grace, we strive to live graciously and gracefully.

We live gracefully by persevering through struggles with uncompromised integrity. "If when you do good and suffer for it

19

you endure, this is a *gracious* thing in the sight of God" (1 Peter 2:20, emphasis added).

We live gracefully when our tone reinforces our faith. "Let your speech always be *gracious*, seasoned with salt, so that you may know how you ought to answer each person" (Colossians 4:6, emphasis added).

We live gracefully when we encourage others. "Let no corrupting talk come out of your mouths, but only such as is good for building up, as fits the occasion, that it may give *grace* to those who hear" (Ephesians 4:29, emphasis added).

We live gracefully when we give. The apostle Paul advocated generosity when he wrote, "As you excel in everything—in faith, in speech, in knowledge, in all earnestness, and in our love for you—see that you excel in this act of *grace* also" (2 Corinthians 8:7, emphasis added).

God's grace alone saves. A Christian's graceful living gives concrete expression to God's sanctifying and sustaining work in us.

People of Grace in the Bible

Search the pages of Scripture and you'll find examples of people responding gracefully to pressure-packed situations. These heroes of the faith reflect the God they served. The Bible describes God as "gracious and merciful, slow to anger and abounding in steadfast love" (Psalm 145:8). God is the author of grace. No one can "out-grace" God. You can't be more graceful than sacrificing Your beloved Son for sinful humanity.

Many times in the Bible, believers faced a crossroads. They could act ungracefully—compromising their convictions, caving in to pressure, holding a grudge, exacting revenge, or repaying hate with hate. Or they could act gracefully—standing firm in their beliefs, showing respect, forgiving, persevering through obstacles, and choosing kindness. On many wonderful occasions, with the help of the Holy Spirit, God's people acted gracefully.

Consider David. King Saul was determined to kill David. On the run, David and his men hid in a cave when the king himself entered, distracted and unsuspecting. The opportunity presented itself. David's men encouraged him to seize the moment and kill the murderous king. David resisted. He sliced off a corner of the king's robe and no more. By rejecting temptation and showing mercy, David exhibited grace under pressure (see 1 Samuel 24).

Consider Daniel. The law was fixed: no praying to anyone except the king. The penalty was clear: a no-return trip to the lions' den. Daniel could have capitulated and conformed. But he held his ground and trusted in God. The king's servants threw Daniel into the lions' den. The man of faith emerged unscathed. By refusing to compromise his beliefs, Daniel exhibited grace under pressure (see Daniel 6).

Consider Queen Esther. Her cousin Mordecai revealed to her a plot to exterminate the Jews. Although it would violate decorum, Esther knew what she had to do: interrupt the king's schedule and alert him. To save her people, she was willing to take the risk. She said, "Then I will go to the king, though it is against the law, and if I perish, I perish" (Esther 4:16). By risking her life to save others, Esther demonstrated courage and resolve (see Esther 4).

Consider Stephen. He was murdered for proclaiming salvation in Jesus. Enraged men hurled stones at him. He could have hurled insults at them. He could have protested. Instead, in his dying breaths, he forgave, saying, "Lord, do not hold this sin against them" (Acts 7:60). By loving his enemies, Stephen exhibited grace under pressure (see Acts 7).

The Graceful Savior

Stephen's words echo Jesus' words from the cross, "Father, forgive them, for they know not what they do" (Luke 23:34). That is where our journey will lead us in this book. The Christian life always leads back to the cross. Without Jesus' death on the cross and His resurrection, we have nothing. By His death and risen life, we have everything. In all of Scripture, the greatest example of gracefulness is our Savior.

On the cross, Jesus was the ultimate example of grace. He didn't lash out at His tormentors. He showed compassion. He *forgave* them. The Bible tells us that Jesus hung on the cross for six hours, from 9:00 a.m. to 3:00 p.m. on that fateful Friday (Mark 15:25, 33–37). Those six hours featured the greatest display of grace ever shown. The majority of this book will explore Jesus' graciousness on the cross, specifically His seven last statements.

On the cross, Jesus was the true source of grace. God's Word teaches that we are "justified by His grace as a gift, through the redemption that is in Christ Jesus" (Romans 3:24). Through the cross, God saves us by grace. Jesus paid the price for our sins. He suffered in our place. By faith in Him, His righteousness is credited to us. That's grace, the most wonderful grace ever shown!

Empowered by the grace of Christ, we seek to live gracefully. Not only does His cross grant us justification through faith, but His cross also leads us to sanctification—that is, holy living inspired by the Savior, who lived in perfect holiness for us. Being graceful under pressure is living out our sanctification.

In Jesus, we have access to an unlimited source of grace. He saves us from our sins. He saves us for holy living. His salvation changes our lives. Even in our hardest moments, He is our strength and our guide. By faith, we have a divine companion in every situation, including the moments that push us to the limit.

Keeping Your Eyes on Jesus

For a modern-day example of being cool under pressure, look no further than Nik Wallenda. Nik is the seventh generation of a family of stunt daredevils and circus performers. He has walked on a steel cable between two skyscrapers in downtown Chicago, across Times Square in New York City, and most famously across Niagara Falls from the United States side to the Canadian side.

In 2020, he topped all his previous stunts by walking on a cable over an active volcano in Nicaragua. It took him thirty minutes to go from one side to the other, crossing over a boiling lake of lava that was spewing toxic gases.

In addition to being an amazing daredevil, Nik is a Christian. In interviews, Nik confesses that he is saved by grace through faith through the cross of Jesus. He says that his faith in God gives him peace in the middle of his death-defying stunts. He could easily be distracted by the danger he's facing. He said he keeps his mind focused on the Lord throughout his stunts, thinking about his faith in God from one end to the other.

The danger around you and me may not be a volcano underneath us. It may be bad news all around us. Or the threat of illness hanging over our heads. Or difficult decisions in front of us. Or our mounting stress within us.

The purpose of this book is to help you fix your eyes on Jesus (Hebrews 12:2 NIV) so that when you face the heat of pressure-packed situations, you can emulate the grace of our Savior. We'll fix our eyes on Jesus by beholding Him on the cross, where He exhibited grace beyond our comprehension. Daily, we face situations that challenge our spiritual composure. You will make it to the other side of your trials. By the power of the Holy Spirit, you can get there gracefully.

Discussion Questions

1. Complete this sentence from your own observations or experiences: Ungraceful behavior is . . .

2. Now complete this sentence: We live gracefully when . . .

3. How can a person be graceful and still be raw and honest about his or her struggles?

4. Choose one of the character studies referenced: David, Daniel, Esther, or Stephen. Read that person's story, as listed in the chapter. Discuss how that story demonstrates graceful behavior.

5. Why do we need the Holy Spirit's help to live gracefully? What does He do that we can't do for ourselves?

6. Review the fruit of the Spirit in Galatians 5:22–23. Which of the fruit do you most desire for yourself right now?

7. If you were to live more gracefully, what effect might that have on the people around you?

8. What do you hope to gain from reading this book?

Therefore let anyone who thinks that he stands take heed lest he fall. No temptation has overtaken you that is not common to man. God is faithful, and He will not let you be tempted beyond your ability, but with the temptation He will also provide the way of escape, that you may be able to endure it.

1 Corinthians 10:12–13

CHAPTER 2

GOD'S PERSPECTIVE ON STRESS

It was 1:30 a.m. Slowly waking from a deep sleep, I missed a phone call. I called back. It was a member of my congregation. She was stressed.

A family issue was weighing on her mind. She couldn't stop thinking about it. She couldn't sleep. She didn't know where to turn, so she turned to her pastor. I was honored that she called.

For several minutes, she poured out her heart. I listened and offered words of comfort. We prayed and said good night.

Can you relate? Stress is real, and it has a real effect on us. It keeps us awake at night. It prevents us from focusing. It steals our joy.

The widespread impact of stress caught my attention years ago after my congregation hosted a conference for professional church workers. We arranged an impressive lineup of speakers, including a famous author who testified that he had died, gone to heaven, and been revived. People were eager to hear him.

But after the conference ended, all the buzz was about a less famous speaker who talked to us about the topic of margin. He said that the margin between our capacity and our workload is shrinking, and as a result, stress is increasing. Conference attendees walked away saying, "He was so right." For many people, his talk hit the bull's-eye.

Signs of the Times

Stressful moments force us to respond one way or another: gracefully or ungracefully. Sometimes we step up and show the best of who God has made us to be. Other times our worst characteristics rise to the surface, and our response is regrettable.

Stress has been called a "national epidemic."[1] Every year, many studies explore the topic of stress. All seem to arrive at the same conclusion: We have a big problem! Consider some signs of societal distress.

This from a study conducted by the American Psychological Association:

- 77 percent of survey respondents regularly experienced symptoms caused by stress

- 48 percent reported lying awake at night due to stress

- 54 percent said stress has caused them to fight with people close to them

- 26 percent said they've been alienated from a family member or friend because of stress[2]

Everyday Health released a report called "The United States of Stress 2019."[3] The report claims that for many Americans today, stress levels are nearly unbearable. Here are some of the report's conclusions:

- Almost one-third of respondents saw a doctor about something related to stress.

- Over half of respondents (52 percent) said financial issues regularly stressed them out.

- Nearly half of all respondents (47 percent) said they react to stress by taking it out on themselves, and that was equally true of both women and men.

The Bible on Stress

At face value, you might conclude that the Bible has nothing to say about stress. Many Bible translations, including the English Standard Version and King James Version, do not include the word *stress* at all. Of the translations that do include the word, none has it more than twice.

This will be a short chapter, right?

Not so fast. Although *stress* is not a common word in our English translations of the Bible, it is a prevalent concept. Hebrew, the primary original language of the Old Testament, includes words commonly rendered as *trouble, anguish, oppressed*, and *distress*. Greek, the original language of the New Testament, speaks of difficult times, anguish of heart, distress, and being hard pressed.

We look to Scripture for understanding because the Bible provides God's perspective. The Bible is an amazing paradox—100 percent God's words and 100 percent human words. Penned by human hands and guided by the Holy Spirit, the Bible says exactly what God wants it to say. It's inspired or "God-breathed" (2 Timothy 3:16 NIV).

Therefore, to get God's perspective on stress, we'll explore several key passages that relate to our topic. For the remainder of this chapter, we'll look at three causes of stress: our own foolishness, personal circumstances, and the world around us.

Foolishness

Our own foolishness produces considerable stress. Proverbs 1:26–27 says, "I also will laugh at your calamity; I will mock when terror strikes you, when terror strikes you like a storm and your calamity comes like a whirlwind, when distress and anguish come upon you." The Christian Standard Bible translation renders the final part of the verse "when trouble and stress overcome you."

Who is saying those words in Proverbs 1:27? "Wisdom" is the speaker. Proverbs 1 depicts Wisdom as saying, "I told you so!" Disregarding Wisdom, the fool ends up mired in distress and anguish. Fools, through ill-conceived actions, bring stress upon themselves.

These two words—*distress* and *anguish*—are two of the most commonly used words in the Old Testament to describe stress. The Hebrew word translated as "distress" is also frequently rendered as "trouble." Have you ever gotten yourself into trouble by foolishly sidestepping wisdom? We all have at some point.

You might recall some foolish choices in your own life. Perhaps it was a purchase that you later regretted. It seemed like such a good deal at the time! Or maybe you rushed a decision instead of taking an extra day to pray about it.

Or your foolish actions might be more severe—so grievous that the thought of them makes your stomach churn: drugs, gambling, pornography, an affair.

All of us make poor choices—some with greater earthly consequences than others. By our own foolishness, we bring stress upon ourselves.

The primary author of Proverbs, Solomon, was intimately acquainted with both wisdom and foolishness. Early in his reign, he requested and received the gift of wisdom. People traveled long distances to hear Solomon's wise teachings.

Over time, Solomon's wisdom diminished. Scripture sadly reports, "For when Solomon was old his wives turned away his heart after other gods, and his heart was not wholly true to the LORD his God, as was the heart of David his father" (1 Kings 11:4). Through foolish choices, Solomon brought stress upon himself and his nation. After all, with seven hundred wives, can you imagine the pressure to remember birthdays and wedding anniversaries!

On a serious note, Solomon faced consequences for his actions. God announced that the kingdom would be torn away from

Solomon's son. God raised up adversaries to oppose Solomon. Tragically, a once-peaceful reign deteriorated.

When we act foolishly, we bring stress upon ourselves. Like Solomon, sometimes we can trace our stress back to our own mistakes.

Circumstances

Another source of stress presented in the Bible is life circumstances beyond our control. First Samuel 1 describes a stressed-out woman. Her name was Hannah. She was unable to conceive, an agonizing disappointment completely beyond her control. As a result of her infertility, Hannah endured ridicule and social pressure.

Her husband, Elkanah, had two wives. Hannah was one; Peninnah was the other. Apparently Peninnah had no trouble increasing Elkanah's family. The Bible speaks of "all her sons and daughters" (1 Samuel 1:4). Peninnah made sure Hannah never forgot who was the "superior" wife. "[Hannah's] rival used to provoke her grievously to irritate her" (v. 6).

Hannah took her grief to the temple. As she prayed in obvious emotional turmoil, the high priest Eli spoke to her. She described herself to him as "a woman troubled in spirit" and said, "I have been speaking out of my great anxiety and vexation" (vv. 15, 16). The New English Translation (NET) renders the word *anxiety* in that passage as "stress."

Hannah was not responsible for her stress, in contrast to the self-induced stress described in Proverbs. Her life condition had created a distressing situation for her.

Maybe you can relate. Perhaps you've been unable to have children, and you worry about a social stigma or being looked down upon. You wish you could change your circumstances, but you can't. Maybe you were born with a disability or an impairment of some kind. You might feel self-conscious, or you might be unable to perform certain activities because of your condition.

You wish you could change it, but you can't do anything about it. You may have grown up in a low-income household. Finances have always been tight, and that has been a burden.

Many situations are handed to us without our asking. They are inherent stresses. We trust in God's plan to demonstrate His strength in our weakness (2 Corinthians 12:9). In that weakness, though, we experience the hardships of living in a broken world.

Godlessness

Another biblical category of stress is problems driven by the culture around us. Paul was concerned that his young protégé, Timothy, may have felt this kind of stress. In 2 Timothy, considered Paul's final biblical letter, the apostle warned that the days ahead would not be easy: "But understand this, that in the last days there will come times of difficulty" (3:1). The Revised Standard Version says, "There will come times of stress" (Greek *chalepos*).

Who wouldn't be stressed by what Paul listed in the next verses?

> **People will be lovers of self, lovers of money, proud, arrogant, abusive, disobedient to their parents, ungrateful, unholy, heartless, unappeasable, slanderous, without self-control, brutal, not loving good, treacherous, reckless, swollen with conceit, lovers of pleasure rather than lovers of God, having the appearance of godliness, but denying its power. (vv. 2–5)**

Yikes!

Paul was describing godlessness in society.

Godlessness in our culture can be a source of stress to us too. On the day I wrote this sentence, a woman approached me on the walkway at church. She said she needed a word of encouragement. I expected her to share a personal trial—maybe a family or financial problem. Instead, she told me she was feeling overwhelmed about everything she was seeing on the news. All the accounts of evil and disruption in society were upsetting her. None of it directly affected her. But she saw so much turmoil in the world, and it affected her.

When we hear about shootings, riots, corruption, greed, and other forms of ungodly behavior, it's distressing. The godlessness that surrounds us can alarm and disturb us. Simply hearing about these things can be enough to raise our blood pressure.

The Promise of Endurance

We've seen in 2 Corinthians 12:9 that God promises grace that is sufficient for us even in weakness. He provides sustaining grace. He sustains us through every stress, whether it's caused by our own foolishness, personal circumstances not of our choosing, or the broken world around us.

The temptation in pressure-packed moments is to give in to our impulses and blow up or melt down. That's the temptation. But it's not the inevitable end result. God also gives us strength to resist sin and to pursue righteous living. In 1 Corinthians 10:13, He promises that "with the temptation He will also provide the way of escape, that you may be able to endure it."

At first glance, we may read "escape" and think we always have the option of side-stepping a problem. But then "endure" appears at the end of the verse. When you endure something, you don't get a free pass. You endure by passing through the dilemma successfully. We aren't able to avoid all problems, but we aren't hopelessly trapped in a corner. God provides an alternative to sin. When tempted, we don't have to compromise God's standards. We don't have to react ungracefully.

God's sustaining grace enables us to pass gracefully through the pressure-packed trials we face. When we're under pressure, by God's strength we resist the temptation to sin and instead respond in ways that honor Him.

Stress doesn't inevitably lead to sin. It didn't for Jesus. Our Lord was the master of enduring pressure-packed situations. The next chapter explores some of the stressful scenarios He faced prior to the cross and how He responded to those pressures. As we consider our own reactions, it's only fair to ask: Did Jesus ever crack under pressure?

Discussion Questions

1. Stress has been called a national epidemic. Do you feel that claim is accurate or an overstatement? Explain your answer.

2. Do you ever sense other people's stress around you? Share an example, if possible.

3. In the chapter, several statistics are cited as evidence of societal distress. Which of the statistics can you relate to most?

4. Do you thrive under deadlines? Or does last-minute work stress you out? How might you deal with someone who's the opposite of you in this department?

5. What causes you more stress: your own foolishness, personal circumstances beyond your control, or godlessness around you? Explain your answer.

6. How do you cope when the cause of stress is outside your control?

7. It has been said that good leaders keep their heads when everyone else is losing theirs. How might you keep your head when others are stressed?

8. How can the group pray for you in the stresses you may be facing currently?

Jesus entered the temple and drove out all who sold and bought in the temple, and He overturned the tables of the money-changers and the seats of those who sold pigeons. He said to them, "It is written, 'My house shall be called a house of prayer,' but you make it a den of robbers."

And the blind and the lame came to Him in the temple, and He healed them. But when the chief priests and the scribes saw the wonderful things that He did, and the children crying out in the temple, "Hosanna to the Son of David!" they were indignant, and they said to Him, "Do you hear what these are saying?" And Jesus said to them, "Yes; have you never read, 'Out of the mouth of infants and nursing babies You have prepared praise'?" And leaving them, He went out of the city to Bethany and lodged there.

MATTHEW 21:12–17

CHAPTER 3

DID JESUS EVER CRACK UNDER PRESSURE?

I t's a shocking scene.

Jesus is flipping over tables. He's dumping coins on the ground. He's driving people out of the temple.

Jesus is doing these things! If your image of Jesus is a meek and mild Savior, this episode will seem completely out of character for Him.

The setting was the temple. Jesus entered and discovered a marketplace inside of God's holy house. Merchants were charging visitors exorbitant rates to purchase temple sacrifices. The merchants' hearts were set on profits, not on God. Jesus once said, "You cannot serve God and money" (Matthew 6:24). The Son of God saw into people's souls, and at the temple that day, He beheld hearts sold out to earthly riches.

So He cleansed the temple, evicting those who had turned God's "house of prayer" into a "den of robbers" (21:13).

The table flipping and coin spilling begs a question. Did Jesus lose His cool? With the exception of John, who may have arranged his stories thematically rather than chronologically, the Gospel writers locate Jesus' cleansing of the temple during Holy Week. Just days away from the crucifixion, did Jesus reach His limit of stress? Was He being ungraceful under pressure?

37

Stress Apart from Sin

First, let's establish this point: Jesus felt stress. He wasn't immune to it. He was truly human—100 percent God and 100 percent man. As man, He had feelings just as we do. External forces affected Him.

One time for a seminary counseling course, I researched how the Bible describes Jesus' feelings. As a class requirement, students had to visit a counselor and experience a counseling session. After we talked, my counselor determined that I was somewhat out of touch with my feelings. He told me to read John's Gospel and analyze Jesus' emotions. I had to underline feeling words with a different colored pen depending on the category: mad, sad, glad, and afraid.

Interesting exercise. I encourage you to try it! I found that Jesus displayed a wide range of feelings. He indeed was fully God *and* fully human!

He felt things, which means He felt stress, as we do. But His stress never led Him to sin. The Bible teaches Jesus' perfect record in many verses:

- He "knew no sin" (2 Corinthians 5:21).

- He was "holy, innocent, unstained, separated from sinners" (Hebrews 7:26).

- "He committed no sin, neither was deceit found in His mouth" (1 Peter 2:22).

Therefore, while He felt stress, He never reacted in a way that violated God's will. He perfectly held the tension between feeling emotions and not letting those emotions control His actions. Ephesians 4:26 says, "Be angry and do not sin." Jesus experienced a wide array of feelings, even anger and frustration. But those feelings did not overpower His self-control. Jesus "in every respect has been tempted as we are, yet without sin" (Hebrews 4:15).

Herein lies a critical distinction between Jesus and us. Often, we react to stress in destructive ways—ungracefully. During His earthly life, Jesus, with masterful self-control, responded to stress in constructive ways.

Note carefully: He did respond to stress. He didn't just stuff it away, trying to ignore it. He was human. He had to release his feelings in some way. No human can keep feelings bottled up forever. The difference is how He responded to stress: not destructively but constructively, in a way that was somehow helpful, instructive, or productive.

Frustrations with Loved Ones

The Gospels are filled with stories of stressful situations in Jesus' life. For the next few pages, let's consider some of these situations, how they compare to our experiences, and how Jesus responded constructively.

Like you and me, Jesus had close relationships with people who at times frustrated Him. His family members thought He was crazy. His hometown neighbors rejected Him. His disciples, the people He spent the most time with during His ministry, were often selfish, clueless, and dense.

I wonder how often Jesus felt stressed over His disciples' shortcomings. Jesus expressed frustration to them with words like, "Are you also still without understanding?" (Matthew 15:16). He pointed out their failure to trust Him completely: "Why are you so afraid? Have you still no faith?" (Mark 4:40). After Peter contradicted Jesus' teaching about His suffering and death—and after Peter had the audacity to rebuke Jesus—Jesus "rebuked Peter and said, 'Get behind Me, Satan!'" (Mark 8:33). Jesus even listened to the disciples argue about who was the greatest among them (Mark 9:33–37).

The people closest to Jesus, the disciples, probably elevated His stress more often than anyone else.

Isn't that how it goes? The people we love the most tend to stress us out the most. Husbands and wives irritate each other. Rebellious children turn their parents' hair gray. Brothers and sisters are best friends one moment and worst enemies the next. The people closest to us can be a significant source of stress. We know them more intimately and see their faults more clearly. And they certainly notice our deficits too.

Jesus felt stress, and He responded to it constructively. He had compassion on His disciples. Rather than write them off as hopeless, He invested in them. He saw their potential and never gave up on them. Repeatedly, Jesus responded to their frustrating comments by launching into a relevant teaching. He recognized their starting point and moved them to greater understanding.

One time, when the disciples were keeping parents from bringing their children to Him, Jesus "was indignant" (Mark 10:14). He could have come unglued. Instead, He turned their misguided actions into a teaching moment, saying, "Let the little children come to Me; do not hinder them, for to such belongs the kingdom of God" (v. 14). In the hands of Jesus, the disciples' error led to greater comprehension of God's kingdom and His love for children.

Oh that the Holy Spirit would grant to us a compassionate spirit for our agitators! Rather than boil over with stress, by God's grace, we can see opportunities for teaching and promoting growth. Sometimes the other person needs to mature and could benefit from your guidance. Sometimes you're the one needing greater understanding, patience, and love. Often, it's a combination of the two, and with the Holy Spirit's help, you grow together.

Criticism

Another source of stress in Jesus' life was criticism. He had enemies. If you're ever discouraged because some people don't like you, you're in good company: people didn't like Jesus!

On many occasions, Jesus' opponents questioned His legitimacy. They argued with Him. They demanded miraculous signs to validate His ministry. They challenged His actions through criticisms disguised as questions, such as, "Why does He eat with tax collectors and sinners?" (Mark 2:16). Real meaning: He shouldn't eat with them.

Criticism applies tremendous pressure. Leaders face this pressure often. Outsiders may not understand why certain decisions are made. From their limited viewpoint, detractors will voice objections, sometimes directed at the decision or action and other times directed at the leader personally. Criticism can be hard to stomach, especially when you've made an honest effort to do your best. With our fragile egos, we tend to forget the ninety-nine compliments and remember only the one negative remark.

If there ever was a principled leader, it was Jesus. Yes, He was criticized. His opponents sought to trap Him. To diminish His credibility with the people, His opponents tried to discredit Him and cut Him down to size.

Under the pressure of criticism, Jesus responded constructively. Rather than react defensively, as if His integrity were questionable, Jesus simply stood on His principles. When the scribes and Pharisees challenged Jesus for His "sinful" dinner companions, Jesus explained the why behind His actions: "Those who are well have no need of a physician, but those who are sick. I came not to call the righteous, but sinners" (Mark 2:17).

When you and I face criticism, we can learn from our Savior by standing on our principles. Your decisions may not always be popular. Sometimes our critics have wisdom to impart, even if those teachings are packaged in a rude way. Rather than react outwardly in a defensive manner or collapse inwardly in self-doubt, we can respond constructively as Jesus did. We can revisit the core convictions that shape our actions. The rest of the world may disagree, but if you're acting in accord with God's Word and living in a principled way, you can withstand unjust criticism with confidence and self-assurance.

Pressure to Perform

Jesus felt the stress of expectations. People demanded much of Him. From the beginning of His ministry, as word spread of His miraculous feats and profound teachings, crowds swamped Jesus. In Mark 1, Jesus healed Peter's mother-in-law, who was ill with a fever. Before the day was over, a line formed to see Jesus: "That evening at sundown they brought to Him all who were sick or oppressed by demons. And the whole city was gathered together at the door" (vv. 32–33).

A whole city gathered! Everyone wanted a favor from Him. He must have felt the pressure of expectations, demands, and desperate hopes. The word *crowd* appears forty-five times in Matthew's Gospel in connection with Jesus' ministry. Surely everyone who came to Jesus seeking a miracle was convinced that his or her problem was the biggest of all and merited His attention.

Sports legend Michael Jordan famously retired three times from professional basketball. The first two retirements were after winning three consecutive championships. In interviews, he has shared that the weight of people's expectations depleted him. Everyone expected him to perform spectacularly every night. Everyone wanted an autograph or a favor. He couldn't leave his hotel room because a mob would engulf him.

You and I may not be sports superstars like Michael Jordan (and we're certainly not Jesus!), but we can feel the pressure to perform. As a pastor, I feel pressure to preach a compelling sermon every weekend. God's faithful people deserve nothing less! You might feel pressure to perform at work. You're striving for a promotion or a bonus. Teachers feel the pressure of children clamoring for attention and parents making demands. Many times, the more you achieve, the more pressure you feel to excel. You don't want to disappoint anyone.

Pressure to perform can burden a person's soul. Surely Jesus felt the pressure. He could have let it overtake Him. He could have tried to please everyone, fulfill every request, and work nonstop until He collapsed from exhaustion. We people-pleasers might go that route.

How did Jesus respond constructively to the stress of expectations? Let's revisit Mark 1. After ministering to the assembled crowd, Jesus went to bed. "Rising very early in the morning, while it was still dark, He departed and went out to a desolate place, and there He prayed" (v. 35).

Jesus did the work, but He also took time to recharge. When we're stressed, we're not at our best. Often, the only way to unwind is to step away from the hustle and bustle. Jesus stepped away, and He prayed.

God made us for a rhythm of work and rest. We work for God by serving our neighbor and fulfilling our vocations. Along with that, God designed us to rest. Rest is so important that the Lord modeled it on the seventh day of creation and established the Sabbath for rest and renewal in God's Word. Like Jesus, we can respond to stressful situations by stepping away and spending time with our Creator, who designed us to rest in Him.

Danger

Physical danger also caused stress in Jesus' life. Like all people, Jesus was vulnerable to danger while inhabiting our human world: attacks by looters and vandals, bad weather, natural disasters, illness, injury. He was in the middle of a storm while at sea (Mark 4:35–41). In Nazareth, an angry mob brought him to the edge of a cliff so they could throw Him down (Luke 4:29). His body was malnourished after forty days of fasting in the wilderness

(Luke 4:1–2). He predicted His death three times, knowing He would not elude death indefinitely (Mark 8:31; 9:30–31; 10:33–34).

Finally, in the Garden of Gethsemane, less than twenty-four hours before His crucifixion, Jesus showed the strain: "And being in agony He prayed more earnestly; and His sweat became like great drops of blood falling down to the ground" (Luke 22:44). His life was in danger. Soon He would suffer pain beyond description. The anticipation of danger elevated His stress level to the point that He sweat blood.

Maybe you've never sweat blood, but you've sweat over the prospect of physical pain or devastation. Surgery is scheduled, and you're a tightly wound ball of anxiety. A surgeon's knife terrifies you. You dread the months of rehab looming.

Unlike a planned surgery, some dangers don't have appointments. You may know the terror of a tornado or hurricane. You may live in a high-crime area, and you worry about your safety. Someone may have threatened to harm you.

Years ago, a church member told me about her "crazy neighbor." His behavior was odd. He said things that made her skin crawl. She felt unsafe in her own front yard. She reported the neighbor to the police, but they could only do so much. She lived in a constant state of anxiety, fearful of her neighbor's unpredictable and erratic behavior. Eventually, she moved—a great relief.

Jesus can relate to the stress of physical danger. Thanks be to God, many dangers we fear never harm us. Not for Jesus. He would not try to escape a public execution. Even if it meant torment, Jesus was committed to saving us by His death on the cross.

Is it possible to respond to physical danger gracefully? First, let me say this: If you're in a physically dangerous situation, get out and get help. Battered women and men need to get away from abusive partners. If you observe dangerous behavior by neighbors or others, please call the police. God does not expect us to remain in a dangerous situation. He cares about our bodies and souls, and He wants us to seek protection when needed.

Jesus' danger couldn't be avoided because God had decreed it. The cross was going to happen. And so Jesus responded constructively to the stress of impending suffering. We, too, can respond constructively to stressful situations, even dangerous ones.

Lessons from the Garden

From Jesus in the Garden of Gethsemane, we observe three constructive measures that apply to all types of stressful situations:

1. **Jesus didn't try to carry the stress alone. He invited His closest friends—Peter, James, and John—to accompany Him.**

2. **Jesus prayed. Prayer calms our souls. It connects us to God, who promises, "My grace is sufficient for you, for My power is made perfect is weakness" (2 Corinthians 12:9).**

3. **Jesus entrusted Himself to His heavenly Father's will. He asked for the cup of suffering to be removed. His request shows just how much angst He felt! While honestly admitting His feelings, Jesus submitted Himself to the Father's plan, praying, "Nevertheless, not My will, but Yours, be done" (Luke 22:42).**

You can respond similarly when under stress. You can enlist others to help carry your burden. You can seek God in prayer. You can entrust yourself to God's perfect will. In all of it, you can trust God, who sent His only Son to suffer in your place so that by faith you would be God's protected child.

Cleansing the Temple . . . in Love?

Let's return to the opening story of Jesus cleansing the temple. Did Jesus lose His cool? Was He ungraceful under stress? No.

Jesus knew exactly what He was doing. Was He emotional? Yes. The Gospels recall Psalm 69:9: "Zeal for Your house will consume me." Jesus was zealous for God's house. He was passionate about honoring what is holy. Emotional responses and sin are not the same thing. Luther wrote, "Zeal is an angry love or a jealous love. . . . [Jesus'] anger does not arise from hatred; it springs from . . . love toward God."[4]

Knowing Jesus, it's entirely reasonable to say that His actions in the temple were done out of love. He turned the tables, but as He did with the disciples, He also turned the moment into a teaching opportunity. Consider the things He said in connection with His actions in the temple.

He reminded them of God's love for all people and His divine mission: "My house shall be called a house of prayer for all nations" (Mark 11:17, quoting Isaiah 56:7).

With all eyes fixed on Him, He leveraged the moment to predict His resurrection: "Destroy this temple, and in three days I will raise it up" (John 2:19).

And look at what Matthew records right after Jesus labeled the scene a "den of robbers":

> And the blind and the lame came to Him in the temple, and He healed them. But when the chief priests and the scribes saw the wonderful things that He did, and the children crying out in the temple, "Hosanna to the Son of David!" they were indignant, and they said to Him, "Do you hear what these are saying?" And Jesus said to them, "Yes; have you never read, 'Out of the mouth of infants and nursing babies You have prepared praise'?" (21:14–16)

He created a stir in the temple by healing and by stirring up the hearts of children to shout His praises.

Jesus knew exactly what He was doing. And He did it out of love for fallen humanity. He was pointing them to Himself as God in human flesh who had come to rescue sinners. The Savior had arrived! "And the Lord whom you seek will suddenly come to His temple; and the messenger of the covenant in whom you delight, behold, He is coming, says the LORD of hosts" (Malachi 3:1).

Jesus dealt with stress purposefully. He responded constructively. Love for humanity always motivated His words and actions.

The pressures He faced leading up to His final hours, while significant, were minor compared to what awaited Him.

A traitor's kiss.

Arrest.

Friends scattering.

Trials.

Slaps. Flogging. Mocking.

Shouts of "Crucify Him!"

Nails. Pounding. Indescribable pain.

The cross.

The moment of Jesus' most agonizing stress had arrived.

The work of salvation had reached its final stage.

Discussion Questions

1. How do you view Jesus' actions in cleansing the temple? Do you find His behavior shocking or out of character? Explain.

2. Jesus felt stress but never sinned. Ephesians 4:26 says, "Be angry and do not sin." What does that verse mean to you?

3. Think of someone who would benefit from you becoming more patient. If you're comfortable sharing, tell the group and ask them to hold you accountable.

4. How do you deal with criticism directed at you? Think of how you might be able to handle criticism better.

5. Do you feel stress because of expectations? Where do the expectations come from?

6. Have you been in physical danger before? Share with the group.

7. Share one practical insight you gained from the chapter and how you plan to apply it in the week ahead.

8. From previous experience, what has helped you to handle stress well?

And when they had crucified Him, they divided His garments among them by casting lots. Then they sat down and kept watch over Him there. And over His head they put the charge against Him, which read, "This is Jesus, the King of the Jews." Then two robbers were crucified with Him, one on the right and one on the left. And those who passed by derided Him, wagging their heads and saying, "You who would destroy the temple and rebuild it in three days, save Yourself! If You are the Son of God, come down from the cross." So also the chief priests, with the scribes and elders, mocked Him, saying, "He saved others; He cannot save Himself. He is the King of Israel; let Him come down now from the cross, and we will believe in Him. He trusts in God; let God deliver Him now, if He desires Him. For He said, 'I am the Son of God.'"

MATTHEW 27:35–43

CHAPTER 4

UNPARALLELED PRESSURE: THE CROSS

Of all the stresses Jesus encountered in His life, none compares to the cross. Nothing even comes close. Human language cannot convey the burden of carrying the world's sins. Think of the worst atrocities ever committed. The Holocaust. The 9/11 attacks. Assassinations, massacres, kidnappings, human trafficking, bombings, rapes. All of it was laid on Jesus. No one ever bore a more unbearable responsibility than Jesus did on the cross.

To grasp the gravity of crucifixion, we have to undo some of our thinking about the cross. In our modern context, the cross has been tamed. We wear cross necklaces. Decorative crosses adorn our walls. Many of the crosses we see are colorful and elegant.

The cross of Jesus was anything but beautiful. It was ugly. Hideous. Despicable in every way. It was an instrument of torture in every sense—not only for Jesus, but also for all crucifixion victims.

Crucifixion in Historical Context

Crucifixion was an ancient form of capital punishment practiced by various societies. From the sixth century BC to the fourth century AD, the Persians, Seleucids, Carthaginians, and Romans executed criminals by crucifixion. Some of the earliest recorded crucifixions occurred in 519 BC, when Persian king

Darius I crucified three thousand political opponents in Babylon.[5] Crucifixion was designed to punish offenders and deter other would-be lawbreakers.

Describing a Roman crucifixion, first-century Jewish historian Josephus wrote: "One of the Jews taken prisoner in this engagement was crucified before the walls, on Titus' orders, in the hope that this sight would lead the rest to surrender in horror."[6] In another passage, Josephus recorded, "When caught, they resisted, and were then tortured and crucified before the walls as a terrible warning to the people within."[7] Along with Josephus, historical figures such as the Roman orator Cicero and the Early Church Father Origen attest to crucifixion as one of the most terrible punishments ever conceived.

For those who witnessed crucifixion, the psychological effect was profound. New Testament scholar N. T. Wright describes it this way:

> **If you had actually seen a crucifixion or two, as many in the Roman world would have, your sleep itself would have been invaded by nightmares as the memories came flooding back unbidden, memories of humans half alive and half dead, lingering on perhaps for days on end, covered in blood and flies, nibbled by rats, pecked at by crows, with weeping but helpless relatives still keeping watch, and with hostile or mocking crowds adding their insults to the terrible injuries.[8]**

In Jesus' day, crucifixion sent an unmistakable message: Don't mess with the Roman Empire. No doubt, anyone considering rebelling against their imperial masters would reconsider any revolutionary intentions.

The cross shook its witnesses to the core. But witnessing it was nothing compared to experiencing it.

While the magnitude of Jesus' crucifixion defies our full comprehension, we can think about the types of misery He experienced. In this chapter, we'll consider three aspects of suffering Jesus endured on the cross: physical pain, verbal abuse, and public humiliation.

Physical Pain

First and foremost, the cross was designed to inflict maximum physical pain. In many ways, Jesus' crucifixion was performed as other crucifixions were. Criminals sentenced to crucifixion first were whipped or scourged. In fact, Jesus' beating began before Pontius Pilate formally sentenced Him to be crucified (John 19:1). The soldiers cruelly compounded the pain by pressing a crown of thorns into the flesh on Jesus' head (v. 2).

Then the condemned person was forced to carry the horizontal beam to the crucifixion site, where the vertical beam already was erected. At first, Jesus carried His own cross (v. 17). But because Jesus' strength was depleted after the brutal beatings, Roman soldiers recruited Simon of Cyrene from the onlookers and forced him to carry Jesus' cross the rest of the way (Matthew 27:32).

At the crucifixion site, a criminal's outstretched arms were bound to the horizontal beam, either tied with ropes or nailed into the wood at the wrists. (A person's hand was considered to extend to the wrist; the wrist bone was a sturdy place to locate a nail.) The nails left their mark on Jesus. After Jesus' resurrection, the disciple Thomas asked to see "in His hands the mark of the nails" (John 20:25).

With the victim affixed, the horizontal beam then was raised and joined to the vertical beam. Ropes or nails fastened the victim to the vertical beam. There the condemned remained until death.

Death was agonizingly slow. The cause of death ultimately could be excessive blood loss or organ failure. Most commonly, death came through asphyxiation as the person's body weight gradually crushed the lungs. Jesus summoned every remaining ounce of strength to cry out "with a loud voice" after six hours on the cross (Matthew 27:50).

Jesus' tormentors spared Him no physical pain. They held nothing back but tortured Him with every imaginable cruelty. Paul writes in 2 Corinthians 13:4 that Jesus "was crucified in weakness." And He was. His body was beaten and battered to the extreme. He died in unspeakable physical pain. He did it all to redeem us.

Verbal Abuse

Along with physical pain, Jesus suffered in another way. His enemies tormented Him with verbal abuse.

If you've ever been verbally attacked, you know the damaging impact of words. The old saying is "sticks and stones can break my bones, but words can never hurt me." We learn quickly that those words aren't true. Jesus suffered through both: the anguish of physical suffering and the sting of hateful words.

People gathered to witness the crucifixion. A small handful were Jesus' supporters: the disciple John; Jesus' mother, Mary; Mary Magdalene; and two other women. A group of women cried over Jesus as He walked to the crucifixion site. Jesus acknowledged those women and spoke to them.

The rest of the crowd, however, had no personal attachment to Jesus. To them, He was a criminal justly punished or at the very least a spectacle. Like the soldiers who mocked Jesus on trial, the crowd around the cross taunted Jesus while He hung dying:

> Those who passed by derided Him, wagging their heads and saying, "You who would destroy the temple and rebuild it in three days, save Yourself! If You are the Son of God, come down from the cross." (Matthew 27:39–40)

But when Jesus spoke of rebuilding the temple, He wasn't referring to a building; "He was speaking about the temple of His body" (John 2:21). Jesus' words were misunderstood and used against Him.

They mocked His claim to be the Son of God. They challenged Him to prove His divinity by liberating Himself from the cross. They were firing cheap shots at a weary, bloodied man in no position to defend Himself.

Jesus' enemies, delighted by the crowd's taunts, added their insults too.

> So also the chief priests, with the scribes and elders, mocked Him, saying, "He saved others; He cannot save Himself. He is the King of Israel; let Him come down now from the cross, and we will believe in Him. He trusts in God; let God deliver Him now, if He desires Him. For He said, 'I am the Son of God.'" (Matthew 27:41–43)

Their taunts were wide-ranging. They considered Him a pointless Savior, unable to save Himself. As the official leaders of Israel, they took exception to His claims of authority. They even mocked His trust in God.

Some of those insults will never fall on us. Savior, King of Israel—no one will accuse us of claiming those titles. But some might mock us for our faith, just as they derided Jesus. We Americans may not be openly persecuted for our faith as in some countries, but we can be harassed and bullied. When words tear us down, we identify with our Savior in His sufferings, saying with the psalmist, "The insults of those who insult You fall on me" (Psalm 69:9 NIV).

Jesus understood what it feels like to be mocked for your faith. He understood the sting of verbal abuse. And He suffered all of it for our redemption.

Public Humiliation

The cross was a deterrent. Crucifixions were conducted in places of high visibility so that witnesses would resolve never to commit a crime of such severity. Jesus was no exception. "It was before your eyes that Jesus Christ was publicly portrayed as crucified" (Galatians 3:1).

Crucifixion made a statement. Part of the statement was, you want to exalt yourself? You want to place yourself above our laws? You want to be high and lifted up? We'll give you high and lifted up! Wright explains,

> Crucifixion thus meant not only killing by slow torture, not only shaming, not only issuing a warning, but also parodying the ambitions of the uppity rebels. They wanted to move up the social scale? Let them be lifted up above the common herd, then—on a cross![9]

Jesus was crucified at "a place called Golgotha (which means Place of a Skull)" (Matthew 27:33). An alternate name is Mount Calvary, derived from the Latin word for Golgotha. Hebrews 13:12 says Jesus "suffered outside the gate," meaning outside the walls of Jerusalem. Anyone passing by could have paused to spectate. Many did.

A component of crucifixion was the psychological battle, waged partly through public humiliation. Executioners dehumanized their victims by stripping away every personal belonging, including clothes, and making criminals a public display of what happens to those who defy the empire.

Nearly all artwork depicts Jesus on the cross with a cloth covering His private area. This is sanitized. Crucifixion victims were not treated with such dignity but were completely exposed. For many reasons, the Bible describes Jesus' crucifixion with words such as "shame" and "offense" (Hebrews 12:2; Galatians 5:11). The treatment of our Savior was sickening.

And He did it all for our redemption.

The Gospels describe in detail what happened to Jesus' clothes, particularly John's Gospel:

> When the soldiers had crucified Jesus, they took His garments and divided them into four parts, one part for each soldier; also His tunic. But the tunic was seamless,

woven in one piece from top to bottom, so they said to one another, "Let us not tear it, but cast lots for it to see whose it shall be." This was to fulfill the Scripture which says, 'They divided My garments among them, and for My clothing they cast lots.'" (19:23–24)

Even in Jesus' public humiliation, Scripture was fulfilled and God was enacting His plan.

On the cross, Jesus took the punishment that we deserve for our sins. We deserve that humiliation. If you've been publicly embarrassed, you know how painful it is. Here's a worse humiliation: Imagine publicly showing off all your mess-ups in life. An unedited replay of our worst moments for all to see would be the most devastating humiliation of all!

Rather than subject us to unending ridicule for our mistakes, God washes away our sins through the blood of the Savior. Instead of labeling us eternally as sinners, He releases us from the burden of our transgressions.

On the cross, Jesus suffered in every way—through physical punishment, verbal abuse, and public humiliation. The word *pressure* doesn't come close to describing what He faced. In speaking of grace under pressure, the point is this: No one has suffered more than Jesus did on the cross. Yet no one has ever responded to adversity more graciously than He did. The words hurled at Him were disgraceful. The words He spoke on the cross were graceful—the ultimate exhibition of grace under pressure.

Discussion Questions

1. Share anything new you learned about crucifixion from the chapter.

2. Why do you think crucifixion was the capital punishment of choice for the Roman government?

3. Do you think the cross has been "tamed" in today's society by its use as art and decor?

4. Describe the worst physical pain you've experienced. What did you say to yourself in the midst of the pain?

5. What do you think motivated the onlookers to verbally abuse Jesus?

6. In today's culture, with social media and other platforms, do you feel that verbal abuse is on the rise? Explain your answer.

7. In the cross, we see the dehumanizing effect of public humiliation. What kinds of truths might help someone who has been humiliated or embarrassed to rebuild his or her self-image?

8. Considering what you read in the chapter, how does it feel to know that Jesus suffered and died on the cross for you?

PART 2

Grace from the Cross

No one ever faced pressure like Jesus did on the cross. The fate of the world was placed squarely on His shoulders. When humanity was at its worst—crucifying the Lord of glory—Jesus was at His best. He gave a master class in grace from the cross, an unmatched display of love. Because of His cross, we receive grace upon grace from God.

And as they led Him away, they seized one Simon of Cyrene, who was coming in from the country, and laid on him the cross, to carry it behind Jesus. And there followed Him a great multitude of the people and of women who were mourning and lamenting for Him. But turning to them Jesus said, "Daughters of Jerusalem, do not weep for Me, but weep for yourselves and for your children. For behold, the days are coming when they will say, 'Blessed are the barren and the wombs that never bore and the breasts that never nursed!' Then they will begin to say to the mountains, 'Fall on us,' and to the hills, 'Cover us.' For if they do these things when the wood is green, what will happen when it is dry?" Two others, who were criminals, were led away to be put to death with Him. And when they came to the place that is called The Skull, there they crucified Him, and the criminals, one on His right and one on His left. And Jesus said, "Father, forgive them, for they know not what they do." And they cast lots to divide His garments. And the people stood by, watching, but the rulers scoffed at Him, saying, "He saved others; let Him save Himself, if He is the Christ of God, His Chosen One!"

LUKE 23:26–35

CHAPTER 5

FATHER, FORGIVE THEM

The moment came and went so fast, Simon Wiesenthal wasn't able to fully process it at the time. But he spent the rest of his life second-guessing what he had done . . . or not done.

Simon was a Holocaust survivor. While he was imprisoned, he was walked through a town where he once lived and brought to a converted hospital to work. As he entered the building, a nurse approached him and asked if he was a Jew. Simon answered yes and was taken to a room.

On a bed lay a dying young Nazi soldier. The Nazi, haunted by his crimes, wanted to confess to a Jew, longing for forgiveness. Simon listened to the man's confession and then, when asked to respond, Simon remained silent.

He said nothing at all. He turned and walked out of the room.

Simon replayed the encounter in his mind endlessly in the years to come. He debated in his mind whether his silence was justified. By saying nothing, he withheld forgiveness.[10]

"They"

Forgiveness doesn't come easily. A more instinctual response is retaliation.

As Jesus hung on the cross, He had His chance. He could have lashed out at His tormentors. Like other crucifixion victims, He could have screamed insults at those who punished Him. Being the Son of God, He could have summoned fire from heaven.

He could have prayed, "Father in heaven, never forget what these people have done to Me. May Your anger burn against them, and may the record of their transgression follow them to the grave."

Instead, He responded completely differently. His words contained no bitterness or anger.

Tradition says that these words recorded in Luke's Gospel were the first Jesus spoke while dying. As Jesus opened His mouth, imagine all the angels in heaven leaning in to hear what He would say. These words set the tone for everything that came after. And remarkably, it was a tone of grace.

"Father, forgive them, for they know not what they do" (Luke 23:34).

Of everything He could have said, He prayed for His Father to forgive them. Let's begin with the second half of the statement: "They know not what they do." Who are "they"?

Are "they" the executioners? These men inflicted unspeakable physical pain. They stretched His bloody back on the splintery cross. They drove spikes into His hands. They hoisted Him into the sky, elevated and exposed for all to see. Jesus had every reason to resent them—to *hate* them.

Are "they" the soldiers standing guard? These men led Jesus from Pilate's presence. Likely, they were among the soldiers taunting Jesus, spitting on Him, whipping Him, and showing no mercy. Jesus had every reason to hate them—to despise them for all the damage they inflicted on His body and psyche.

Are "they" the crowd who turned against Him, yelling, "Crucify Him"? No greater insult had ever been given. They chose a convicted criminal over Jesus. They demanded the release of Barabbas and sentenced Jesus to death. Jesus had every reason to desire that they feel the sting of rejection that He felt.

Are "they" the religious and political leaders responsible for His sentencing? Really, they were at fault. For months, the Jewish leaders had conspired against Jesus. Jealousy consumed them. Their insecurity and thirst for power compelled them to eliminate Jesus.

All those are possible answers. Speaking of God's wisdom in the cross, Paul wrote, "None of the rulers of this age understood this, for if they had, they would not have crucified the Lord of glory" (1 Corinthians 2:8). In their ignorance, all these people had Jesus' blood on their hands. All were complicit. None were innocent.

One more possibility for "they know not what they do"? It could describe all of humanity, including us.

Our sins drove those nails into His hands. *We* know not what we do. Especially in our stressed-out reactions. When the pressure is mounting and we blow up. When we make disastrous decisions that we'd never make under normal conditions when we're thinking straight. In so many cases, we sin, not knowing what we do. We're the ignorant ones.

Spiritual Ignorance

In many places, the Bible speaks of humanity's spiritual blindness. Scripture contains numerous laments over what people don't know. It grieves the Lord when we don't know the ways of peace (Isaiah 59:8), the ways of the Lord (Jeremiah 5:4), how to do right (Amos 3:10), the thoughts of the Lord (Micah 4:12), or the righteousness that comes from God (Romans 10:3). In our ignorance of these things, we sin against God and one another.

So often ignorance is at the root of sin. We know not what we do.

Many times, we veer off course, and we're oblivious it's happening. The religious leaders of Jesus' day? They thought they were doing the right thing. They were convinced they were serving the Lord. Others have been duped by similar delusions. Nazi loyalists thought they were doing the right thing—defending their rights, supporting a nationalistic cause. The 9/11 terrorists were convinced of their rightness. They justified murder as jihad—a holy war.

On a less extreme level, conflict flares up routinely when two parties are each convinced they're doing the right thing. Republicans and Democrats—many see themselves as good guys and their opponents as bad guys. Family members pick sides in an argument, persuaded that their side is the right side.

All the while, we have blind spots. We dig in our heels and fight without understanding the other person's point of view. We don't see the weaknesses of our argument. Our perspective is limited, but we press on as if we had the complete picture.

In the case of Jesus' tormentors, they lacked the whole picture. They didn't know what they were doing because they didn't know what God was doing. The Romans were clueless. Their religious system gave them no reference point to a Messiah, a promised Savior. The Jewish leaders, however, had clues. They had the Old Testament prophecies. In Acts, Paul declared, "For those who live in Jerusalem and their rulers, because they did not recognize Him nor understand the utterances of the prophets, which are read every Sabbath, fulfilled them by condemning Him" (Acts 13:27). At Jesus' birth, Magi from the East interpreted the prophecies and came to worship the true King. Why didn't Jesus' own people?

In fairness to the Jewish leaders, how many of us would have recognized Jesus as the promised Savior? Even Jesus' disciples struggled to grasp His identity fully. The ignorance that plagued the leaders was ignorance of their own sin, their own insecurities, their own selfish motives.

In ignorance, Jesus was crucified.

And yet Jesus pleaded, "Father, forgive them."

Intercessor

Curiously, Jesus asked His Father to forgive. How different. In His ministry, Jesus personally forgave people. One time a woman of ill-repute entered a house and poured perfume on Jesus' feet. Jesus' hosts made clear who she was. Unfazed, Jesus spoke directly to the woman, "Your sins are forgiven" (Luke 7:48). To which His hearers responded, "Who is this, who even forgives sins?" (v. 49). His words sparked contention: Only God could forgive sins! When Jesus directly forgave sins, jaws dropped in disbelief.

On the cross, however, Jesus didn't forgive sins directly but asked His Father to do it. Why is that? Was Jesus trying to be less offensive? At this point, I can't imagine that He was picking His words based on other people's misguided opinions.

Technically, in His first words from the cross, Jesus wasn't forgiving directly. Jesus was *interceding* for them. He was pleading for His tormentors to be forgiven. He was using His divine clout to advocate for bloodthirsty men who had beaten Him, shoved thorns into His head, mocked Him, and nailed Him to the cross. Talk about a graceful request!

A distinction can be made that forgiveness is for the repentant and intercession is for the unrepentant. Jesus died to earn forgiveness for all people. But not all people receive His forgiveness. A calloused heart resists forgiveness. In most cases, it's counterproductive to speak forgiveness to someone who is not sorrowful. True reconciliation is a transaction of sorrow and grace.

Jesus' audience wasn't repentant. Not yet. They thought they were doing a good thing, punishing a criminal and troublemaker. And so Jesus interceded for them, asking His Father to pardon them. In doing so, Jesus fulfilled messianic prophecy: "Therefore I will divide Him a portion with the many, and He shall divide the spoil with the strong, because He poured out His soul to death and was numbered with the transgressors; yet He bore the sin of many, and makes intercession for the transgressors" (Isaiah 53:12). And Jesus did all of this while in unfathomable pain. When people were at their worst, Jesus was at His best.

"Intercessor" is one of the most wonderful descriptions of who Jesus is and what He does for us. In His earthly ministry, Jesus interceded for others. He assured Peter, "I have prayed for you that your faith may not fail" (Luke 22:32). As He agonized in the Garden of Gethsemane, sweating blood during intense prayer, Jesus asked His heavenly Father to grant unity and spiritual protection to all believers, saying, "I am not praying for the world but for those whom You have given Me, for they are Yours" (John 17:9). Even before the cross, our Savior was interceding for us in prayer. Now, as our ascended Lord, Jesus is advocating for us: "Christ Jesus is the one who died—more than that, who was raised—who is at the right hand of God, who indeed is interceding for us" (Romans 8:34).

Even in those moments when we're blind to sins, Jesus has us covered. Even when we act out of stress instead of love, Jesus speaks to the Father in our defense. "If anyone does sin, we have an advocate with the Father, Jesus Christ the righteous. He is the propitiation for our sins, and not for ours only but also for the sins of the whole world" (1 John 2:1–2).

Loving Your Enemy

Jesus teaches us the path of intercession. People might hurt you and never feel sorry. They might be convinced of their rightness, even when God's Word is clear about their sin. Or people may be oblivious to the harm they've inflicted, and repentance never occurs to them. We may never be reconciled to everyone completely. But we can intercede for others, including our enemies. Regardless of their mindset, ours can be fixed on God's ways. We can be graceful by asking God to forgive them.

This is not easy! It can be extremely difficult to desire good for our tormentors. Sometimes we'd rather pray for our enemies with words similar to a country song titled "Pray for You." Inspired by a preacher's encouragement to pray for others, the artist thinks about how to apply the sermon to his relationship with his ex-girlfriend. Here are some of his petitions:

I pray your birthday comes and nobody calls
I pray you're flyin' high when your engine stalls
I pray all your dreams never come true

Just know wherever you are, honey, I pray for you[11]

Praying for your enemies is just the opposite of those words! Interceding for your enemies aligns with God's Word in Romans 12:21: "Do not be overcome by evil, but overcome evil with good."

Jesus lived out His own words to "love your enemies and pray for those who persecute you" (Matthew 5:44). When you pray in love for your enemies, you diminish any power they have over your heart. By faith in Jesus, the God of grace rules in our hearts. His reign is evident when we resist our natural impulses—when we overcome evil with good.

What might you say to God when you pray for your enemies? Pray for wisdom for how to interact with him. You can't control anyone but yourself. Pray for God to soften her heart. Pray for God to resolve whatever is irritating him or setting her on edge. Pray for your enemy to forgive you, and pray for the grace to forgive him. Pray for a miracle of relational healing, and trust in the God of miracles. The first step in loving your enemy is praying for those who persecute you.

Jesus did. It's one of the lessons of grace under pressure that He teaches us from the cross. When we pray for our enemies, a burden leaves our shoulders and rests on the shoulders of the Savior, who can endure the greatest strain. He proved it on the cross.

Discussion Questions

1. What does Jesus' first statement from the cross teach us about our Savior?

2. How does ignorance lead to sin?

3. Should people be considered responsible for sins committed in ignorance? Why or why not?

4. Tell about a time you interceded or advocated for someone else. How about a time when you did this for someone who sinned against you?

5. The chapter made a distinction between forgiveness and reconciliation. How can we feel at peace if we're not completely reconciled with another person?

6. What does it look like to overcome evil with good?

7. How can your small group intercede in prayer for you this week?

8. Based on what you read in this chapter, how can you be a person of grace this week?

And the people stood by, watching, but the rulers scoffed at Him, saying, "He saved others; let Him save Himself, if He is the Christ of God, His Chosen One!" The soldiers also mocked Him, coming up and offering Him sour wine and saying, "If You are the King of the Jews, save Yourself!" There was also an inscription over Him, "This is the King of the Jews." One of the criminals who were hanged railed at Him, saying, "Are You not the Christ? Save Yourself and us!" But the other rebuked him, saying, "Do you not fear God, since you are under the same sentence of condemnation? And we indeed justly, for we are receiving the due reward of our deeds; but this man has done nothing wrong." And he said, "Jesus, remember me when You come into Your kingdom." And He said to him, **"Truly, I say to you, today you will be with Me in paradise."**

LUKE 23:35–43

CHAPTER 6

YOU WILL BE WITH ME IN PARADISE

In 1894, a church was constructed in Kingston, Ontario, just down the road from the Kingston Penitentiary. Its exterior was limestone quarried, cut, and transported by convicts. The first clergyman there also served as prison chaplain, and many of the church members were prison employees. The parish was named the Church of the Good Thief.

It wasn't named in honor of the convicts who built it. It was named in tribute to a thief crucified next to Jesus. In some Christian traditions, he's called St. Dismas. If you look closely at the Church of the Good Thief, you'll see a statue of St. Dismas on the front of the church, a monument to God's surprising grace.

Fittingly, Jesus died as He lived: among sinners. During His lifetime, Jesus was criticized for eating and drinking with sinners. On the cross, He died with sinners. Crucified between two thieves, Jesus was "numbered with the transgressors," as Scripture foretold (Isaiah 53:12).

The thieves responded to Jesus in completely opposite ways. One joined the chorus of taunts directed at Jesus. The other believed, and his soul was saved. As theologian Fulton Sheen wrote, "The thief died a thief, for he stole paradise."[12] If there's hope for that thief, there's hope for all of us in Jesus.

The story of Jesus and the thief on the cross is arguably the most comforting story in the Bible. It's a story of grace—God's amazing grace, which transforms sinners into saints.

Recognizing the King

If not for the life-changing power of God, the story never would have happened. Matthew's Gospel tells us that at first, both criminals were hurling insults at Jesus: "And the robbers who were crucified with Him also reviled Him in the same way" (27:44). You might expect that behavior from a thief. Jesus was the exception—a peaceful, innocent victim. Usually the cross was reserved for the most hardened criminals.

Some speculate that the two thieves next to Jesus were associates of Barabbas, the intended occupant of the middle cross. The other two criminals could have been Barabbas's accomplices in a horrendous crime. The repentant thief openly admitted their guilt, saying to the other thief, "Do you not fear God, since you are under the same sentence of condemnation? And we indeed justly, for we are receiving the due reward of our deeds" (Luke 23:40–41). They deserved punishment, and he knew it. By all appearances, it was too late for the thief. His life was all but over. Because he lived his life apart from God, his eternal doom was sealed. Or so it appeared, until he met Jesus.

Jesus was different. He responded to the stress and pain differently. He was graceful, not vindictive. He sought forgiveness for His enemies. No doubt, the thief would have observed Jesus' words and behavior. And the thief would have noticed the sign over Jesus' head, which read, "This Is the King of the Jews" (v. 38).

The sign was intended as a mockery of Jesus and an insult to the Jewish leadership. Leading up to a crucifixion, it was common for the criminal charge to be written on a sign placed around the criminal's neck or carried next to him on the road. The charge against Jesus was sedition. His opponents claimed that He was inciting rebellion against the Roman Empire.

Hearing the accusation, Pontius Pilate wrote the inscription. The chief priests, Jesus' accusers, argued against Pilate's wording, saying, "Do not write, 'The King of the Jews,' but rather, 'This man said, I am the King of the Jews'" (John 19:21). Pilate responded firmly, "What I have written I have written" (v. 22). The exchange between Pilate and the chief priests drips with irony. Pilate allowed himself to be bullied and blackmailed into sentencing Jesus to death. He lacked backbone then. But when challenged over the sign, Pilate stood his ground on something far less consequential.

Pilate may have intended the sign as mockery, but God used it for evangelism. The thief noticed the sign that declared Jesus to be king. Beneath the sign, the thief saw a man suffering gracefully for a cause. The man was wearing a crown made of thorns, dripping with blood. *Who is this man?* the thief must have thought. *He forgives His enemies. He's a king but suffers like a common criminal. Who is this man?*

Miracle of Conversion

Seeing how Jesus handled Himself differently, the thief then acted accordingly. The insults ceased. The hate evaporated. Something stirred inside of him. The Holy Spirit began to move within him. While suffering his own excruciating pain, the man cried out, "Jesus, remember me when You come into Your kingdom" (Luke 23:42). He knew what he deserved: punishment for his evil deeds. But he boldly asked for more than he deserved, more than any of us deserve. After all, he had nothing to lose and everything to gain. And that's what happened. He gained everything.

What a radical transformation. One minute he was a condemned thief, a lost soul, far away from God. The next minute he was heaven-bound.

Why did one thief come to faith and not the other? Why were the presence and word of Christ effective in one heart but not the other? The answer to that mystery belongs to God. Both thieves had knowledge of Jesus. Both had proximity to Him. One believed. For one, intellectual knowledge registered in the heart and elicited a cry for salvation. The man's last prayer may have been his first prayer.

You might be praying for the Holy Spirit to turn a loved one to Jesus. You may be praying for a miraculous conversion. Your prayers are not in vain! Why some believe and others don't— that's a mystery. Whether we should pray for the salvation of others—that's not a mystery. Jesus taught His followers "always to pray and not lose heart" (Luke 18:1). Our loved ones' eternal destinies matter to us; think how much more they matter to God, who sent His Son to die for them and "who desires all people to be saved and to come to the knowledge of the truth" (1 Timothy 2:4). When we pray for others, we extend God's grace to them.

Promise of Paradise

God desires the salvation of all. For that reason, Jesus gave the repentant thief the gift of eternal life. Jesus' second statement from the cross was, "Truly, I say to you, today you will be with Me in paradise" (Luke 23:43).

You might wonder why Jesus said "paradise" and not "heaven." He could have spoken either word to refer to eternal life with God. But *paradise* had a particular connotation. The word has its roots in the Persian kingdom. *Paradise* literally meant a "walled garden." In the ancient world, honored subjects were invited to stroll with the king through the majestic gardens of his palace.

Jesus promised the thief a place of honor in the heavenly kingdom. Revelation 2:7 describes heaven in this way: "To the one who conquers I will grant to eat of the tree of life, which is in the paradise of God." Spending eternity with God *is* paradise.

On what basis did Jesus make this marvelous promise? On the basis of faith. The thief may be remembered as the good thief. But he really wasn't good. He had a good moment on the cross.

One brief moment of goodness couldn't possibly compensate for a lifestyle of thievery, could it?

No, the thief's best moment couldn't earn paradise. None of our best moments can. But Jesus did.

Salvation isn't a contest between our bad deeds and good deeds. It's a contest between Jesus and everything that opposes God. Salvation is not our triumph. It's Jesus' triumph. It's His victory over sin, death, and the devil. Jesus promised the thief paradise because paradise was Jesus' possession to give. Jesus didn't promise paradise because the thief was good. Jesus promised paradise because *Jesus* is good. The thief really wasn't the good thief. He was the redeemed thief.

Because of God's grace, the thief received better than he deserved. As he said to the unrepentant thief, they were receiving the "due reward" for their deeds. Because of their crimes, under Roman law, both thieves deserved the death penalty. What they deserved extended even further. As sinners, they deserved the eternal punishment of hell. All sins ultimately are transgressions against God.

The Problem with Fair

In Jesus' second statement from the cross, we see this mark of grace under pressure: Jesus gave the thief better than he deserved. Jesus gave the man paradise. It was a gift—100 percent grace.

Sometimes we become discouraged when we feel deprived of what we "deserve." We complain about the injustice of being passed over for a promotion or a bonus. We seethe when someone else gets the credit even though we did most of the work. We recoil as we witness misguided people getting away with treachery. Life isn't fair!

When I think of the word *fair*, my mind goes back to eighth grade Sunday School. I distinctly remember my teacher saying that "fair" was a concept the serpent introduced in the Garden of Eden to create jealousy in the hearts of Adam and Eve. "God knows everything and you don't. Not fair! Eat the fruit so that your eyes will be opened."

Certainly, fairness and equity are staples of a just society. But when it comes to our relationship with God, thank the Lord He's not fair! He's better than fair. If we got what we deserved in our relationship with God, we'd be separated eternally because of our sin. Our sinful nature and our willful rebellion against our Maker merits eternal punishment. The Bible teaches, "Cursed be everyone who does not abide by all things written in the Book of the Law" (Galatians 3:10), and, "The wages of sin is death" (Romans 6:23).

That's what our deeds deserve, but Jesus gives us better than what we deserve! The rest of Romans 6:23 reads, "But the free gift of God is eternal life in Christ Jesus our Lord." As Jesus gave eternal life to the repentant thief, He gives the same gift to you and me. And in both cases—ours and the thief's—eternal life is completely a gift.

Being graceful under pressure means setting aside our presumed right to exact retribution. It's not our place to decide what others deserve. Those judgments belong to God. Instead of basing our actions on what others deserve, we can act based on what *God* deserves. He deserves our very best, always.

What God Deserves

In a preview of heaven, the Book of Revelation includes songs acclaiming God as "worthy." In Revelation 4–5, one song magnifies God as Creator and two songs exalt Jesus as Redeemer. The third "worthy" song says, "Worthy is the Lamb who was slain, to receive power and wealth and wisdom and might and honor and glory and blessing" (5:12). Jesus' work on the cross has merited these things and infinitely more!

What if we approached life with this mindset? Rather than give others what we think they deserve, we treat them according to what God deserves. *He* is worthy. He deserves our very best. Our lives are a response to His grace on the cross. When we love and forgive others, we're giving God what He deserves, a life of grace lived in gratitude to Him.

Even when others show us their worst side, we can give them our best. As redeemed sinners, our lives are a response to our Savior. He is worthy of more kindness than we could ever demonstrate.

Discussion Questions

1. What does Jesus' second statement from the cross teach us about our Savior?

2. What comfort do you find in the story of the redeemed thief?

3. What does the story teach us about the nature of God's grace?

4. Have you ever struggled with the concept of life being unfair? Please share.

5. Tell about a time when you received better than you deserved.

6. How can you give others better than they deserve?

7. Whose conversion can you pray for?

8. Based on what you read in this chapter, how can you be a person of grace this week?

When the soldiers had crucified Jesus,
they took His garments and divided
them into four parts, one part for each
soldier; also His tunic. But the tunic was
seamless, woven in one piece from top
to bottom, so they said to one another,
"Let us not tear it, but cast lots for it to
see whose it shall be." This was to fulfill
the Scripture which says, "They divided
My garments among them, and for My
clothing they cast lots." So the soldiers
did these things, but standing by the
cross of Jesus were His mother and His
mother's sister, Mary the wife of Clopas,
and Mary Magdalene. When Jesus saw
His mother and the disciple whom He
loved standing nearby, He said to His
mother, **"Woman, behold, your son!"**
Then He said to the disciple, **"Behold,**
your mother!" *And from that hour*
the disciple took her to his own home.

John 19:23–27

CHAPTER 7

BEHOLD, YOUR SON; BEHOLD, YOUR MOTHER

Next to the original Good Friday when Jesus died, April 14, 1865, is arguably the saddest and most famous Good Friday in history, at least for Americans. That's the day John Wilkes Booth fired a bullet into the head of President Abraham Lincoln during a show at Ford's Theater.

April 14 is remembered as the day of Lincoln's assassination. However, he didn't die until the next day.

At the theater, several doctors immediately attended to the mortally wounded president. Needing a bed for him but not wanting to move him too far, a group transported Lincoln to the nearby home of William and Anna Petersen. The president was laid in a back bedroom. As Lincoln lay there dying, more than ninety people came to pay their final respects.[13] Among the visitors were Lincoln's wife, son, and cabinet members.

Then, at 7:22 a.m. on Holy Saturday, April 15, 1865, the sixteenth president of the United States died.

As Jesus was dying on the original Good Friday, the circumstances were different. Jesus was not lying horizontal on a cushioned mattress; He was suspended vertically on a splintery wooden cross. No one offered Him medical care; no one came to His aid. As far as Scripture tells us, nowhere close to ninety people visited Him to pay their final respects. Only a tiny group of loyal followers assembled at the cross.

Jesus' final supporters were a faithful few: "Standing by the cross of Jesus were His mother and His mother's sister, Mary the wife of Clopas, and Mary Magdalene" (John 19:25). Jesus' weary eyes focused on two people. The next verse adds that Jesus "saw His mother and the disciple whom He loved," which is how John referred to himself (v. 26).

In the small group, that's who Jesus noticed. Out of the women gathered there, He saw His mother. Out of all the disciples gathered, He saw John.

Wait a minute. Out of all the disciples? No other disciples are mentioned at the cross. The others were AWOL. At Jesus' arrest in the Garden of Gethsemane, "they all left Him and fled" (Mark 14:50). The other disciples lost their courage. Out of the group, John alone returned to Jesus at the cross.

Only a privileged few are invited to gather around a person's deathbed. In this case, Mary and John responded to the Holy Spirit's invitation to stand at the foot of the cross. You could argue that these were the two most significant relationships in Jesus' earthly life. Mary brought Him into the world, nursed Him, bathed Him, clothed Him, and loved Him as only a mother can. John was Jesus' steadfast friend—the beloved disciple—part of the inner circle of friends who accompanied Jesus to the Mount of Transfiguration and the Garden of Gethsemane.

Seeing Mary and John, Jesus spoke His third statement from the cross: "He said to His mother, 'Woman, behold, your son!' Then He said to the disciple, 'Behold, your mother!'" (John 19:26–27).

Picture it. Jesus is suffering indescribable pain. Yet He's thinking about others! His focus is not on His agony. His focus is on the needs of His mother and best friend. What presence of mind! What compassion! What grace!

All about Me

Jesus' attention to Mary and John astounds. Under the most intense stress ever experienced, our Lord's pressing concern was the well-being of His mother and friend. On our best days, we're not as servant-minded as Jesus was on His most awful day.

Because of our sinful nature, we're inwardly focused. In confirmation class, I teach the students that in the middle of *sin* is the letter *I*. Jesus tells us to love God and love our neighbor because those things don't come naturally.

Our sinful nature convinces us that life is all about me! As a playful parody, a media company made a spoof church video for an imaginary congregation called Me Church. The church's slogan: "Where it's all about you." Here are some of the perks of joining Me Church:

Running late? No problem. Church starts when you arrive!

Fussy baby? Not to worry. You stay in your seat. Everyone else can leave![14]

I was disappointed the church didn't offer customized temperature control for your section of the pew!

Our nature is to focus on ourselves. Instead of "How can I serve others?" the question becomes "How can others serve me?" We take our eyes off others and their needs and become absorbed only with our own needs. Our primary thoughts become what do people think about *me*? What's best for *me*? How do *I* get what *I* want? How do *I* win, even if it means that others lose?

Grace doesn't factor into that mindset . . . unless it's other people showing grace to *me*!

Roots of Selfishness

Where does this inward focus originate? Is it picked up by hanging out with the wrong crowd and watching the wrong TV shows? No. Its roots are much more fundamental. We're born that way, "brought forth in iniquity" (Psalm 51:5).

Think about babies. Let me be clear: I love babies. My wife and I have been blessed with four precious children. But if you've been around babies, you know that their focus is *me*! Feed *me*!

Change *my* diaper! Rock *me* to sleep! You can't fault babies. They can't care for themselves, so they cry for help.

The problem is that we never grow out of our self-focus. It stays with us. And while we can excuse cute babies for demanding constant attention, adults aren't so adorable when we make life all about *me*. By being selfish, babies reveal their neediness. That's understandable. When adults are selfish, we reveal our sinfulness.

Selfishness begins at infancy and, left unchecked, grows like a weed. Martin Luther, in teaching about infant Baptism, wrote,

> **If a year ago someone was proud and greedy, then he is more proud and greedy this year. So the vice grows and increases with him from his youth up. A young child has no special vice. But when it grows up, it becomes unchaste and impure. When it reaches maturity, real vices begin to triumph. The longer the child lives, the more vices. Therefore, the old man goes unrestrained in his nature if he is not stopped and suppressed by Baptism's power.**[15]

God gives us a wonderful gift in Baptism! He refuses to allow our selfish, sinful nature to dominate. To combat our inward focus, He unites us to Christ through water and the Word so that our thoughts, words, and actions more closely resemble His. Through the Holy Spirit within us, we're able to get outside of ourselves and place our attention on God and the people He has given us to serve.

Maintaining an outward focus in not easy. Some days it can be an incredible struggle. But God helps us in the struggle. We can pray for God to make us more Christlike in living out the words of Philippians 2:4: "Let each of you look not only to his own interests, but also to the interests of others." When we concern ourselves with others' needs, our goal becomes what's best for them. Not what they deserve. Not what we feel like giving them. But what is best for them. Often, meeting their needs requires grace.

A Mother's Grief

That's exactly what Jesus did: In the most excruciating pain, He was looking out for the interests of others. Other people were chief in Jesus' mind. After all, that's why He came into the world—not for Himself, but to serve and save humanity. In His third statement from the cross, we see our Savior's unshakable outward focus. In those words, He was looking out for Mary and John.

As Jesus hung on the cross, most certainly the person who weighed heaviest on His heart was Mary. No one would grieve more deeply than Mary. The other day, I spoke to a member of my congregation whose adult son died a few weeks before. I asked how she was handling the loss. One thing she said: "I wish I still could have my son here. But I believe our children are on loan from God. Ultimately, they're His." What a faith-filled perspective. May God strengthen the faith of all moms and dads who grieve the loss of a child. I can't imagine a worse grief.

Although she couldn't have known exactly how it would happen, it's likely that Mary anticipated a day of intense pain. When Jesus was eight days old, Joseph and Mary brought Him to the temple. The Law of Moses required parents to present their newborns to the Lord. A seasoned believer named Simeon prophesied to Mary, "Behold, this child is appointed for the fall and rising of many in Israel, and for a sign that is opposed (and a sword will pierce through your own soul also)" (Luke 2:34–35). Even from infancy, the shadow of the cross hung over Jesus . . . and, in a sense, over His mother.

Nothing would prevent the pain of losing her firstborn son. Mary would have to endure the sorrow as Jesus accomplished God's plan for our salvation. Jesus ensured, however, that Mary's suffering would not be compounded by material deprivation. As a woman in first-century eastern culture, Mary would struggle financially without the provision of a man. Women did not have the same rights and privileges as men. They couldn't earn income the way men could. Many widows descended into poverty.

Jesus' death would leave a huge void in Mary's life, not just emotionally but also in her family structure. Most scholars assume that her husband, Joseph, had already died. Scripture last mentions Joseph when Jesus was age 12 (see Luke 2:41–52). Some may ask, "Why didn't Jesus entrust Mary to one of His brothers?" Here's the thing: John believed in Jesus, but Jesus' brothers did not, at least not until the resurrection. John 7:5 says that "not even His brothers believed in Him." Jesus wanted to make sure His mom had material provision *and* spiritual support in her journey of grief.

A Best Friend's Loss

Jesus entrusted His mother to His closest friend, John. Jesus' life was filled with people. He had many friends, but some were closer than others. After His resurrection, He visited 500 supporters (1 Corinthians 15:6). After His ascension, 120 believers bonded together (Acts 1:15). He sent out 72 for ministry (Luke 10:1). Then there were the twelve disciples. Within the Twelve was an inner circle of three: Peter, James, and John. Finally, among the three, John was "the disciple whom Jesus loved" (John 13:23; 21:7, 20).

At the Last Supper, John was the one "reclining at table at Jesus' side" (John 13:23). When John asked who would betray Jesus, our Lord confided in him that it would be the man to whom Jesus handed a morsel of bread. Then Jesus gave the bread to Judas.

After the resurrection, Peter seemed to scoff at the notion that he would die a martyr's death, but Jesus didn't predict a similar fate for the beloved disciple. Peter asked, "Lord, what about this man?" (John 21:21). Jesus had a special purpose for John, who lived to old age and wrote several New Testament books, including his Gospel, three letters, and the Book of Revelation.

John's closeness to Jesus can be seen in the beloved disciple's writings. John wrote from his unique perspective as Jesus' closest friend, someone who saw Jesus in His most glorious and most painful moments.

From all we know, Mary was Jesus' closest family relationship, and John was His closest friend.

Linked by Faith

By linking Mary and John together, Jesus formed a bond between two people who were equally yoked spiritually. Both were people of strong faith.

Thirty-three years before, as a faith-filled young girl, Mary accepted the angel's word that she, a virgin, would conceive and bear a son. Now, decades later, she stood at the cross while the unspeakable happened—her Son's murder.

Note this word from the biblical text: she was *standing* at the cross (John 19:25). She was not crumpled to the ground in despair. The Bible says she was *standing*. By courageous faith, she was standing. Ephesians 6:13 says, "Take up the whole armor of God, that you may be able to withstand in the evil day, and having done all, to stand firm." By His powerful Spirit, God granted a strong faith to Mary throughout her life. In providing for her future, Jesus ensured that someone would be with her to bolster her faith.

John also was strong in belief. It took faith and courage for him to be there too. Remember Mark's words: "They *all* left Him and fled" (emphasis added). Everyone fled, including John. But John alone returned to Jesus. It takes courage when you've failed someone to come back. John's return displays faith. He had faith that Jesus could forgive his betrayal. He had faith that it wasn't too late for grace.

John was right. Jesus had grace for him, just as Jesus has grace for all of us. No sin is too enormous for Him to forgive. Each of us deserts Jesus when we sin. When we hurt others, we turn our backs on Jesus and His ways. Nonetheless, Jesus never disowns us. He invites us to His cross to find forgiveness and acceptance, as John found.

And so, Jesus entrusted His mother and best friend to each other. They were linked to strengthen each other in the days and years ahead.

This is how God works. He puts people together to strengthen one another. I suppose He could simply impart spiritual strength by zapping it into us. But more often than not, He works through people as conduits of His consolation. Scripture says God "comforts us in all our affliction, so that we may be able to comfort those who are in any affliction" (2 Corinthians 1:4). God strengthens people through people. Mary and John. Moses and Aaron. Naomi and Ruth. David and Jonathan. Elijah and Elisha. Mary and Elizabeth. Paul and Barnabas. God provides for the needs *of* His people *through* His people.

By bringing people together, God provides ongoing opportunities to forget ourselves and consider others. Instead of spiraling downward in grief and self-pity, Mary gained another "son" to love with motherly devotion. Instead of drifting wayward without his Friend and Guide, John could seek wisdom from Mary and perform the duties of a male protector and provider. Fulfilling Jesus' dying wishes, "from that hour the disciple took her to his own home" (John 19:27).

Noticing People

While saving humanity from sin, Jesus wasn't too busy to notice individuals. Jesus was redeeming the world. He was accomplishing the most important act of all time. Even then, He wasn't too occupied with saving the world that He couldn't notice people and their needs. Jesus' love for you and me is just as personal. He notices you.

How good are you at noticing others? So often, we're consumed with our own problems that we fail to recognize the struggles of others. Commit today to forget yourself and be more mindful of others. Don't just make it your goal. Make it your prayer! The Lord hears your prayer. He's able to establish that mark of grace in you: even under pressure, focusing not primarily on *me* but on him or her or them.

Discussion Questions

1. What does Jesus' third statement from the cross teach us about our Savior?

2. Use your imagination for a fun question. If Me Church really existed, what do you hope it would offer?

3. What helps you to forget about yourself for a moment and attend to others' needs?

4. What do you make of the fact that Mary was *standing* at the cross? In this regard, how is she an example to us?

5. Why do you think John was the only disciple at the cross? What did he have to overcome personally to be there?

6. Mary and John both experienced intense grief over the loss of a son and best friend. What has helped you to deal with grief?

7. The chapter lists pairings of believers who supported one another. Besides a spouse, tell about someone God has given you for mutual encouragement.

8. Based on what you read in this chapter, how can you be a person of grace this week?

*Now from the sixth hour there was
darkness over all the land until the
ninth hour. And about the ninth hour
Jesus cried out with a loud voice,
saying, "Eli, Eli, lema sabachthani?"
that is, "**My God, My God, why
have You forsaken Me?**" And some
of the bystanders, hearing it, said,
"This man is calling Elijah." And one
of them at once ran and took a sponge,
filled it with sour wine, and put it on
a reed and gave it to Him to drink.
But the others said, "Wait, let us see
whether Elijah will come to save Him."*

MATTHEW 27:45–49

CHAPTER 8

WHY HAVE YOU FORSAKEN ME?

Why?
It's the universal word of confusion, disorientation, and searching. In times of trouble, a burning question is, "Why, Lord?"

"Why did that happen to him?"

"Why is she going through this?"

"Why now?"

"Why me?"

Throughout the pages of the Bible, people asked God the same thing: "Why, Lord?"

When Pharaoh refused to release God's people, Moses asked God in frustration, "Why did You ever send me?" (Exodus 5:22).

After crossing the Red Sea, when the people's complaining exhausted him, Moses asked God, "Why have You dealt ill with Your servant? And why have I not found favor in Your sight, that You lay the burden of all this people on me?" (Numbers 11:11).

In the promised land, reeling after military defeat, Joshua asked, "Alas, O Lord God, why have You brought this people over the Jordan at all, to give us into the hands of the Amorites, to destroy us?" (Joshua 7:7).

The psalmists wrote: "Why, O Lord, do You stand far away? Why do You hide Yourself in times of trouble?" (Psalm 10:1). "Awake! Why are You sleeping, O Lord? . . . Why do You hide

Your face? Why do You forget our affliction and oppression?" (Psalm 44:23, 24).

Perhaps you've had your own why questions. Maybe you've endured a season of life when you wished for answers and understanding but instead felt clueless. Most often, our why questions arise, as the psalmist wrote, from affliction and oppression.

Out of all the why questions, Jesus' stands alone. This question revealed the extent of Jesus' suffering for our sake. This question exposed the impact of the cross on God the Father and His beloved Son. It's the why question that outweighs all others.

"My God, My God, why have You forsaken Me?" (Matthew 27:46).

For many people, this question prompts another: What exactly was happening between God the Father and God the Son when Jesus was on the cross? Several theories have been offered to explain what exactly was happening to Jesus when He spoke His question. Let's examine three prominent theories.

What Was Happening?

The first theory is that as Jesus took the sins of the world on Himself, God the Father had to turn away, and Jesus felt the Father literally forsaking Him. The Bible says that "for our sake He [God the Father] made Him [God the Son] to be sin who knew no sin, so that in Him we might become the righteousness of God" (2 Corinthians 5:21). This theory claims that in the exact moment of Jesus' anguished cry, God the Father poured out on Jesus all the sins of humankind, from the beginning to the end of time. In that moment, fellowship between God the Father and God the Son was shattered, leaving Jesus alienated, abandoned, dying alone on the cross. God is holy, separate from sin, absolutely pure. Thus, when Jesus absorbed the world's sins, God the Father could not remain in fellowship with Him.

The second theory says that the first interpretation takes too literal a view of Jesus bearing the world's sins. What exactly would God have placed on Jesus? And is it possible for God—who is omnipresent, everywhere at all times—not to be present at any moment? Those who hold this view believe that Jesus' question from the cross demonstrates His humanity. He was experiencing what we might feel to a lesser degree: a time when God appears to have forsaken us. Pain and doubt overtake us and block out any sense of God's presence. When Jesus came into this world, He took on our human nature. "Since therefore the children share in flesh and blood, He Himself likewise partook of the same things, that through death He might destroy the one who has the power of death, that is, the devil" (Hebrews 2:14). Jesus was 100 percent God and 100 percent human. He felt anything we can feel. As He hung on the cross in indescribable pain, He felt completely alone, forsaken by God the Father, though the Father didn't literally abandon Jesus.

The third theory suggests that Jesus' question from the cross was directed not toward God but toward those listening. It was less a question and more a declaration of His identity and purpose. As in the other statements from the cross, Jesus was concerned about those who watched and heard Him. In the first statement, Jesus asked God the Father to forgive His tormenters. In the second, Jesus promised eternal life to the thief beside Him. In the third, Jesus entrusted Mary and John to each other. Might it be possible that even in His question of anguish, Jesus was mindful of His audience? Could it be that in this moment, He was showing grace under pressure by speaking words for the benefit of others?

Jesus' fourth statement was an Old Testament quotation, the opening of Psalm 22. Matched only by Isaiah 53, Psalm 22 vividly prophesies the suffering Savior: "A company of evildoers encircles Me; they have pierced My hands and feet—I can count all My bones—they stare and gloat over Me; they divide My garments among them, and for My clothing they cast lots" (vv. 16–18). Guided by the Holy Spirit, King David composed those words . . . a millennium before Jesus lived as a human!

The third theory about Jesus' why question suggests that He was connecting Himself to the prophecy. He was announcing that He was suffering in accordance with the prophecy. Jesus became sin for us so that our sins would not separate us from God. He experienced indescribable pain to spare us from eternal torment. He died to fulfill the concluding words of Psalm 22: "All the ends of the earth shall remember and turn to the LORD, and all the families of the nations shall worship before You. For kingship belongs to the LORD, and He rules over the nations" (vv. 27–28).

Words of Suffering

Which theory is correct? It may not be necessary to choose one. Each has value. Each underscores a different facet of what was occurring on the cross. Yes, Jesus carried our sins. Yes, He felt the pain of abandonment by God. Yes, He fulfilled the depiction of a tortured man in Psalm 22. All these descriptions point to a singular truth: Jesus suffered unimaginable agony on the cross.

Jesus' first three statements relate to the theme of grace. His fourth and fifth reinforce the theme of pressure. In the fourth statement and the events surrounding it, we see the intense pressure—pressure that no one but the Son of God could endure. He truly suffered for our sake.

Jesus suffered in darkness. In the Bible, darkness is synonymous with evil. Jesus said, "People loved the darkness rather than the light because their works were evil" (John 3:19). When soldiers arrested Jesus in the garden, our Lord remarked, "This is your hour, and the power of darkness" (Luke 22:53).

On Good Friday, the ultimate darkness descended. A truly innocent man was unfairly tried, condemned, and executed. As the light of the world was dying, the world was darkening— literally. Right before Jesus' cry of abandonment, the Gospel writer reports, "Now from the sixth hour there was darkness over all the land until the ninth hour. And about the ninth hour, Jesus cried out with a loud voice, saying 'Eli, Eli, lema sabachthani?' that is, 'My God, My God, why have You forsaken Me?'" (Matthew 27:45–46).

Nature was protesting the injustice. One commentator writes, "The sun hid its face at noon, as if ashamed to shed its light on the crime men committed at Calvary."[16] The darkness in the sky gave physical expression to the darkness Jesus experienced at the hands of sinful men. The Creator of the heavens and the earth suffered alone in darkness.

Jesus suffered in contempt. His loneliness was magnified when the bystanders misinterpreted His words and mocked Him. This is one of the few times the Greek New Testament includes transposed Aramaic speech, which is what Jesus spoke. Jesus' actual spoken words were, "Eli, Eli, lema sabachthani?"

Hearing "Eli," His listeners mistakenly believed Jesus was calling Elijah. Little did they know, Jesus had met with Elijah on the Mount of Transfiguration days before. Certain that Jesus was crying out in vain to a long-departed prophet, the bystanders jeered, "Wait, let us see whether Elijah will come to save Him" (Matthew 27:49). The absence of a heavenly rescue reinforced the sad reality: No one was going to save Jesus. No one would speak up in His defense. Only voices of contempt reverberated in the darkness on Mount Calvary.

Jesus suffered in isolation. His greatest suffering had nothing to do with the darkness in the sky or the mocking voices. His most searing agony was not in relation to nature or people. His most intense pain was in relation to His heavenly Father. It's one thing for the sun to hide itself, for trusted friends to scatter, and for enemies to disparage Him. It's another thing entirely for the Holy Trinity to be in disharmony and for Jesus to feel the full impact of God-forsakenness.

In John 10:30, Jesus said, "I and the Father are one." No one ever experienced such unity as Jesus and His Father, who with the Holy Spirit exemplify the perfect relationship of love and mutual support. On the cross, Jesus suffered in relation to God—an unprecedented event.

Never Forsaken

You may relate to some extent. It might feel like darkness has overtaken your life. The sun still shines in the sky, but your heart and hopes have grown dim. The painful events of life—the kind that provoke those desperate why questions—have dragged you down to the deepest depths of discouragement.

Years ago, many people were stunned to read excerpts from a book of letters written by Mother Teresa. Mother Teresa was one of the most admired Christian leaders of the twentieth century, famous for her tireless work among the poor of Calcutta, India. Her letters revealed instances when she felt tormented spiritually and doubted her faith. The letters became known as her "dark letters." She wrote about the suffering within her, a deep loneliness, an unrelenting inner pain, a sense that everything in her was dead. She wrote that she felt separated from God and compared her sufferings to the tortures of hell. She asked others to pray for God to give her courage as she fought through her own spiritual weakness.[17]

Yes, even a godly woman of renowned faith struggled with spiritual darkness.

Your darkness may have descended because of a death in the family. Or the loss of a job, and with that job, the loss of identity and purpose. Or a decision that has haunted you. Or words of another person that have lodged in your mind, invading your thoughts.

You may have encountered contempt from others, as Jesus did. Perhaps someone has criticized you relentlessly. Maybe your words, like Jesus' words, have been misinterpreted, and you've been misunderstood. Perhaps people have belittled you.

Like our Savior, we at times suffer in darkness and contempt.

But one thing differs: You never have to fear God-forsakenness. Jesus experienced alienation from His Father so that you and I never would. That was the purpose of the cross. Our sins separate us from God, but by atoning for our sins, Jesus brings us to God as spotless, forgiven children of our heavenly Father.

The promise of God's Word covers you in this life and eternity: "I will never leave you nor forsake you" (Hebrews 13:5). And the risen Lord issues His personal guarantee, "Behold, I am with you always, to the end of the age" (Matthew 28:20).

In those times when questions outnumber answers, we look to the cross and remember that God never abandons us. His grace sustains us in the darkness. By His presence, the darkness around us is never greater than the light within us. Through Christ in us, we can maintain a posture of grace and spiritual composure.

We also look to the cross—to Jesus' question on the cross—and learn from His words. Even in pain, the words convey faith. Note what is repeated in the question: "My God, My God." In their times of darkness, first the psalmist and finally Jesus still claimed, "You are *my* God." In times of disorientation, heartache, and inner turmoil, we know that He remains "*my* God."

As He has promised, "You shall be My people, and I will be your God" (Jeremiah 30:22).

Darkness may descend. Friends may bail. Enemies may taunt. God may seem silent. But none of that changes the fact that God is my God and your God—the God of all who trust in the finished work of Jesus on the cross.

Ultimately, the answer to the why question is "who." Who can help when all else falls apart? Who can sustain us with grace that propels us forward?

Jesus.

We look to our Savior, who never forsakes us but abides with us always.

Discussion Questions

1. What does Jesus' fourth statement from the cross teach us about our Savior?

2. Are "Why, Lord?" questions productive? Why or why not?

3. The chapter presents three theories about Jesus' question from the cross. Which of the theories resonates with you most?

4. If you were present that day, what might you have interpreted Jesus' fourth statement to mean?

5. What is your reaction to Mother Teresa's "dark letters"? How do her struggles compare with your struggles?

6. Read Psalm 22. What words or phrases stand out to you? How does it remind you of Jesus? Do any words or phrases connect to your life experiences?

7. What difference does it make in your life to know that God will never forsake you?

8. Based on what you read in this chapter, how can you be a person of grace this week?

After this, Jesus, knowing that all was now finished, said (to fulfill the Scripture), "I thirst." A jar full of sour wine stood there, so they put a sponge full of the sour wine on a hyssop branch and held it to His mouth.

John 19:28–29

CHAPTER 9

I THIRST

In the hot Texas summers where I live, it's important to stay hydrated. You can't go wrong with good old-fashioned water, and you also have drinks specifically designed to replace lost nutrients. The leader in sports drinks is Gatorade. In America, 142 bottles of Gatorade are sold every second.[18] In the sports drink industry, the company holds a market share of more than 70 percent.[19]

Dr. Robert Cade created Gatorade in 1965. Dr. Cade taught internal medicine at the University of Florida. An assistant coach for the Florida Gators approached Cade about the problem of football players becoming dehydrated in the scorching temperatures and oppressive humidity of the deep South. Cade and his research assistants tried several experimental drinks with the football players, and through those experiments settled on the formula for Gatorade, named because of its connection with the Florida Gators.[20]

Interestingly, Dr. Cade hails from my tribe—he was a Missouri Synod Lutheran. One of my seminary buddies did his vicarage, or internship, at First Lutheran Church in Gainesville, Florida— Dr. Cade's church. Cade was on his church's shut-in list, and my friend Landon brought him Holy Communion at home. Months after my friend's vicarage ended, Dr. Cade died at age 80. Landon said the Gatorade founder was a strong Christian, committed to His Lord. Dr. Cade, who quenched the thirst of millions, had his deepest thirst quenched by Jesus.

Spiritual Thirst

One time Jesus expressed His thirst to a woman standing at a well.

> **Jesus said to her, "Everyone who drinks of this water will be thirsty again, but whoever drinks of the water that I will give him will never be thirsty again. The water that I will give him will become in him a spring of water welling up to eternal life." (John 4:13–14)**

Jesus came to be the great thirst-quencher.

You may know what spiritual thirst is like. We all have dry seasons. Times when God seems distant. Times when life perplexes. Times when setback after setback deflates our spirits. David authored Psalm 63 while in the desert, literally and figuratively. Listen to his opening words: "O God, You are my God; earnestly I seek You; my soul thirsts for You; my flesh faints for You, as in a dry and weary land where there is no water" (v. 1). Ever felt that way? Spiritually parched? Emotionally weary? Drained deep within? Spiritually thirsty, we stagger through desert times, acutely aware of our weakness.

Other times, spiritual thirst is subtler, like dehydration. Dehydration surprises us. You're outside working in the yard for hours. You feel fine. But when you go inside and sit down, you realize you forgot to drink anything. Then you feel unwell. Your mouth is sticky. You're weak. Your head throbs. Dehydration sneaks up on us. Spiritual dehydration ambushes us too.

I was listening to a sermon the other day. The pastor confessed, "I've been out of town for a little while. I need to tell you why. I was getting burned out and needed to get away. It has been an intense few months of ministry. I was running hard. All of a sudden, it just hit me like a ton of bricks. I was depleted and didn't have anything else to give. I needed to get away." Quite an admission. Spiritual dehydration ambushed him.

Spiritual dehydration reveals itself through symptoms—many times, through ungraceful living. A short temper. Persistent worry. Growing guilt. Increasing fear. You notice yourself spiritually dry, and you didn't see it coming. A few days without prayer. A couple of weeks without reading your Bible. We neglect to hydrate our souls, thinking we're fine. But all of a sudden it becomes obvious you're not okay. You're suffering from spiritual dehydration.

Just as the body suffers without water, the soul shrivels when we're disconnected from the living water, Jesus. As the Lord said through the prophet Jeremiah, "My people have committed two evils: they have forsaken Me, the fountain of living waters, and hewed out cisterns for themselves, broken cisterns that can hold no water" (2:13). When we forget about God and attempt life on our own, our spiritual dehydration eventually shows.

Jesus' Thirst

Jesus came to quench our spiritual thirst. To do that, He experienced thirst. His fifth statement from the cross is brief: "I thirst" (John 19:28). And no wonder! He'd been on the cross for six hours in the hot Middle Eastern sun. Prior to that, He had been on trial—passed back and forth between the authorities—for perhaps another six grueling hours. After all that, He needed a drink!

He turned down a drink once before. As He walked to Golgotha, some people offered wine mixed with myrrh, but Jesus refused it. The drink was a sedative designed to dull the agony. Jesus was resolved to drink the cup of suffering His Father had poured for Him.

Far from a sedative, what Jesus drank on the cross would extend life and therefore prolong pain. It was a cheap, sour wine consumed by soldiers. And Jesus drank it.

In reflecting on Jesus' thirst, some commentators spend a lot of time analyzing Jesus' words as a metaphor. They write about

Jesus' thirst for justice or thirst for unrequited love. And those things are true. Jesus thirsted for justice, and God's demands for justice fell on Jesus! Jesus thirsted for love. His life was an expression of love for humanity, but humanity rejected His love.

The metaphorical approach can highlight Jesus' priorities as our Savior. But when He said, "I thirst," from the cross, it was more than an analogy. His thirst was physical suffering. In this fifth statement from the cross, we see the humanity of Jesus. Truly, "the Word became flesh" (John 1:14). The infinite took on a finite human body.

He was fully God and fully human. He had human emotions. Sometimes His eyes welled with tears of grief. He became hungry. No doubt His stomach growled when empty. He needed sleep. Once He was so tired He slept through a fierce storm. He got sick. He endured puberty. He probably smashed his finger assembling furniture in his father's carpentry shop.

He was human for our sake. He took on our human nature to redeem us. Our high priest sympathizes with us in our weakness (Hebrews 4:15). Saving the world squeezed Him dry, down to the last drop.

All was finished; Jesus would declare it in His next words. He obeyed His Father's will perfectly to the end. Nearing the completion of His mission, Jesus received this final drink to fulfill Scripture: "My tongue sticks to My jaws" (Psalm 22:15) and "For my thirst they gave me sour wine to drink" (Psalm 69:21).

Some theologians suggest that Jesus accepted the drink because He needed to moisten His mouth to speak His final two statements. He wanted to ensure that His final words came out clearly. He would conclude His act of atonement only after declaring its completion.

Hearing of His thirst, the soldiers extended the sour wine to Him on a hyssop branch. The Israelites used a hyssop branch to paint lamb's blood above their doorposts on the first Passover as Moses prepared to lead the people out of Egypt. And now the Lamb of God had come to atone for all sins. According to

Hebrews 9:19–20, after Moses spoke the Commandments, "he took the blood of calves and goats, with water and scarlet wool and hyssop, and sprinkled both the book itself and all the people, saying, 'This is the blood of the covenant that God commanded for you.'" By His death, Jesus ushered in the new covenant of forgiveness by His blood (Matthew 26:28). In God's perfect plan, it all came together. For you. For me. For our salvation.

Quenching Our Thirst

On the cross, Jesus thirsted so that by the cross our spiritual thirst would be quenched. When we place ourselves at the foot of the cross, we find renewal. Jesus said, "I am the vine; you are the branches. Whoever abides in Me and I in him, he it is that bears much fruit, for apart from Me you can do nothing" (John 15:5). A healthy branch is connected to the vine. From the vine, hydration and nutrients flow into the branch. Apart from the vine, the branch withers. When we are connected to Jesus through His Word, through Holy Communion, through prayer, His life-giving power flows into us.

During the COVID-19 pandemic, like many churches, my congregation worked hard to keep people connected to Jesus through Word, Sacrament, and prayer. We invested in livestreaming equipment to broadcast worship services online. We wanted our members and community to hear the Gospel, whether in person or at home. We offered a Communion service in the parking lot. Each Sunday morning, a dedicated group of volunteers assembled our "outdoor worship center," including a sound system and elevated pulpit (i.e., decorated scaffolding). There in the parking lot, people received the true body and blood of Jesus for the forgiveness of their sins.

One evening inside the church building, we hosted a prayer vigil structured around the petitions of the Lord's Prayer. We prayed for the medical community. We asked for protection from the virus. We interceded for our nation's leaders. We pleaded for an end to discrimination and racial unrest.

Why all these efforts? They were designed to keep people connected to Jesus through Word, Sacrament, and prayer. Without staying firmly connected to the vine, branches wither. Living things suffer from malnourishment. Our spirits suffer without nourishment from our Lord.

Just as dehydration shows itself in its symptoms, so also proper hydration shows itself. Gatorade achieved national prominence after the Gators came from behind to win the Orange Bowl against Georgia Tech in 1967. Afterward, Georgia Tech head coach Bobby Dodd told reporters, "We didn't have Gatorade. . . . That made the difference."[21] Whether or not Coach Dodd saw the Florida Gators drinking Gatorade on the sidelines, he saw the results in their energetic performance. He saw the difference it made.

People can see the difference when we're spiritually hydrated and when we're not. A spiritually hydrated Christian exhibits greater peace, more joy, and a serving spirit. A spiritually hydrated Christian is graceful under pressure, like our Lord was on the cross. What Jesus did for us on the cross—God's plan of salvation—was specifically engineered to give us life and revive our weary souls.

Jesus said, "If anyone thirsts, let him come to Me and drink. Whoever believes in Me, as the Scripture has said, 'Out of his heart will flow rivers of living water'" (John 7:37–38). Refreshed by Jesus, you can be a river of love, encouragement, and hope. Jesus makes the difference for us, and He wants to make the difference for others too.

Jesus is the difference, especially in moments of weakness. When all our strength is sapped, He remains strong within us. When we're feeling spiritually dry, He revives us. He abides as our source of life and hope. Without Him, we shrivel up. With Him, we flourish!

Discussion Questions

1. What does Jesus' fifth statement from the cross teach us about our Savior?

2. When you need to rehydrate, what's your preferred drink?

3. From your own experience, what are signs of spiritual dehydration?

4. On a scale of 1 to 10, how spiritually hydrated are you right now? Explain your answer.

5. The Bible says Jesus is our high priest who sympathizes with us in our weakness. (Hebrews 4:15). What does that statement mean to you personally?

6. How did you stay connected to your church or faith community during the COVID-19 pandemic?

7. How can you tell that you're staying spiritually hydrated? What attitudes or actions give evidence of spiritual health in your life?

8. Based on what you read in this chapter, how can you be a person of grace this week?

When Jesus had received the sour wine,
He said, "It is finished," and He bowed
His head and gave up His spirit.

John 19:30

IT IS FINISHED

One of the all-time great masterpieces was created by a reluctant artist who quit in frustration at the end. Michelangelo was a sculptor by trade. At age 33, he was working on a marble tomb when the pope asked him to paint the ceiling of a brand-new chapel. The artist balked at first but finally relented. He spent the next four years painting on scaffolding, often miserable from physical discomfort and doing something he didn't really want to do.[22]

The pope didn't make it any easier. In a biography of Michelangelo written by one of his students, we learn what it was like behind the scenes. Pope Julius was an impatient man, prone to micromanaging. Many times he would pull up a ladder next to Michelangelo. The artist would give the pope a hand and help him onto the scaffolding. Eager to showcase the work to the public, the pope would ask Michelangelo to unveil parts before he had done the finishing touches. This always irked the artist.

After finishing the Sistine Chapel, Michelangelo vented to his student that the work wasn't finished as he had hoped. The pope's constant pressure had become unbearable. One day, the pope asked when the chapel would be finished. The irritated artist brushed him off, saying, "When I can." The pope replied, "Do you want me to have you thrown off the scaffolding?" At that, Michelangelo stepped down from the scaffolding and had it disassembled. The project ended at that moment. The pope had wanted the painting retouched with gold. Michelangelo had no interest in continuing. He was done. It was finished.[23]

Enough Is Enough?

On the cross, Jesus spoke, "It is finished" (John 19:30). It's possible to read those words as "I've had enough." For thirty-three years, the Son of God endured life among sinful humanity. He was a perfect person among imperfect people. He was God, the author of the Ten Commandments, living among nonstop commandment-breakers. Surely thirty-three years as a man must have tested Jesus' patience. One time, Jesus said in exasperation, "O faithless and twisted generation, how long am I to be with you? How long am I to bear with you?" (Matthew 17:17). Despite the frustrations, Jesus never quit.

At the end, however, He was pushed harder than ever before in His thirty-three years.

At the end, Jesus endured misunderstandings, accusations, and verbal abuse. His friends, the disciples, misunderstood Jesus and His mission. His enemies, the jealous religious leaders, looked for every opportunity to catch Jesus making a false move. They persuaded the governing authorities that Jesus was a threat to society. Jesus stood by silently as His opponents leveled accusation after accusation against Him. They assigned impure motives to Him. They convinced the crowd that a murderer named Barabbas deserved freedom and the author of life deserved death. People used the power of words against the Word made flesh. Enough already!

Jesus absorbed beatings, pierced hands and feet, and the anguish of slow suffocation on the cross. Soldiers, trained men of strength, pounded away at Him. He felt the nails ripping through His skin and tissue. He struggled to breathe as His body sagged. The physical pain was unbearable. Enough already!

Jesus saw His tormentors smiling with satisfaction.

He suffered the indignity of being publicly executed between two thieves.

He watched his mother and best friend in deep emotional pain at the foot of the cross.

He felt abandoned by God.

In the hot Middle Eastern heat, His thirst was unbearable.

At this point, it would be perfectly understandable if Jesus' shout from the cross was "Enough already! I'm done! *It is finished!*"

Not a Quitter

But Jesus wasn't a quitter. He was graceful under pressure all the way to the end. He wouldn't throw in the towel in frustration. He wasn't going to crack under pressure and abandon His mission. He would not give up.

Ever wanted to give up? I have. I hate to admit it, but it's true. At times, I've felt completely defeated.

Thank the Lord for friends who have come alongside me when my spirit was crushed. Some of their words resound in my ear to this very day. I can hear one spiritual mentor saying, "Stay in the fight." I can hear another saying, "Stay the course." Stay with it. Stick with it.

God's Word teaches perseverance: "Let us not grow weary of doing good, for in due season we will reap, if we do not give up" (Galatians 6:9). If you're doing a good thing, that good thing needs to continue despite adversity. All of us grow tired and weary. Weariness in doing good is not a sign to give up. It may be a signal to take a break, but not to give up. We trust that God will bring about His harvest of blessings in due season.

Don't give up.

Perhaps the most compelling passage about perseverance is Hebrews 12:1–2:

> Therefore, since we are surrounded by so great a cloud
> of witnesses, let us also lay aside every weight, and sin
> which clings so closely, and let us run with endurance

> the race that is set before us, looking to Jesus, the founder and perfecter of our faith, who for the joy that was set before Him endured the cross, despising the shame, and is seated at the right hand of the throne of God.

We run our race with endurance because Jesus ran His race with endurance. He never gave up. He looked beyond the cross to the joy set before Him—the joy of His resurrection and the joy of our salvation. Keeping His eyes on the prize, He endured the cross.

We see Jesus' remarkable endurance when we carefully examine His sixth statement. Jesus did not say, "*I am* finished." His words did not indicate defeat or exhaustion. His words were something entirely different.

Reaching the Goal

"It is finished." In the Greek, it's one word, *tetelestai*, from the root *telos*, as in telescope. A telescope looks ahead. *Telos* refers to a goal. *Tetelestai* is the word for when you submit the final assignment of your college career. It's the word for when you pay your final mortgage payment. It's the word for when you cross the finish line of your first half-marathon. It means, "I successfully completed the work I set out to do." "It is finished" was not a cry of defeat. It was a shout of victory!

Jesus accomplished exactly what He came into this world to do. He came to bear our sins and be our Savior.

All His life led to this moment on the cross. The baby born in Bethlehem entered the world for the purpose of dying on the cross. He lived to die.

All His miracles were signs pointing to Him as the Savior. Onlookers were astonished when Jesus prefaced a miracle with a declaration of forgiveness. Before healing a man who was paralyzed, Jesus said, "But that you may know that the Son of Man has authority on earth to forgive sins . . . I say to you, rise, pick up your bed and go home" (Luke 5:24). The miracles pointed to Jesus as Savior, the Son of Man, whose ultimate purpose was to forgive sins.

All His teachings demonstrated His authority—authority by which He would lay down His life and take it up again, as He says in John 10:18. On at least three occasions, He declared unambiguously that He would suffer, die, and rise again. In the parable of the wicked tenants (Luke 20:9–18), He foreshadowed His sacrifice. He was the beloved son, killed by greedy men. He taught with an eye toward the cross.

Jesus' goal was to pay the price for our sin. He never gave up on that goal and remained focused on it to the very end. Talk about grace under pressure!

Perfect Life

"It is finished." What exactly was finished? What is "it"? "It" has two sides. Theologians call these two aspects of Jesus' atoning work His active and passive obedience. Active obedience refers to His perfect fulfillment of God's Law. Jesus is the only person in history to obey all of God's commandments without failing once. In fact, He's the only person to make it through a single day without breaking a commandment.

I recently came across this prayer:

Dear Lord,

So far today, I'm doing all right. I have not gossiped, lost my temper, been greedy, grumpy, nasty, selfish, or self-indulgent. I have not whined, cursed, or complained. But I will be getting out of bed in a minute, and I think that I will really need Your help then.[24]

We need God's help! Every day is a challenge greater than we can handle alone. In our weakness, we stumble and fall into sin.

The Bible teaches that Jesus did what we could not: "For we do not have a high priest who is unable to sympathize with our weaknesses, but one who in every respect has been tempted as we are, yet without sin" (Hebrews 4:15). By resisting sin flawlessly, Jesus perfectly obeyed His Father's will.

But Jesus' life wasn't only about avoiding sin, and neither are our lives. If the purpose of life were to avoid sin, each of us should hide in our homes and never leave! Life also is about actively doing good. It's about serving. Jesus served others with unparalleled love. By resisting evil and choosing good actions, Jesus was the perfect sacrifice for us. "For as by the one man's [Adam's] disobedience the many were made sinners, so by the one man's [Jesus'] obedience the many will be made righteous" (Romans 5:19).

Along with avoiding sin and actively serving, Jesus' active righteousness also uniquely includes everything He did to fulfill Scripture. The word *tetelestai* is used only twice in John's Gospel. Once is in Jesus' words from the cross. The other time is two verses prior. Jesus came to fulfill the messianic prophecies. He knew His active obedience was completed when the Scriptures were fulfilled. John 19:28 says Jesus prepared for His death, "knowing that all was now *finished*" (emphasis added). He had done everything.

Perfect Sacrifice

Passive obedience refers to Jesus paying the price for our sins through His suffering and death. Sin has consequences. Jesus took the eternal consequences of sin upon Himself. He was the sacrifice that a holy God demands in payment for sin.

Oswald Chambers wrote in his devotional book *My Utmost for His Highest*, "God forgives sin only because of the death of Christ. . . . Never allow yourself to believe that Jesus Christ stands with us, and against God, out of pity and compassion, or that He became a curse for us out of sympathy for us. Jesus Christ became a curse for us by divine decree."[25]

I find the phrase "divine decree" interesting. God already had decreed that a sacrifice was needed to atone for sin. The Old Testament describes a detailed system of animal sacrifices. Different animals were sacrificed in different ways depending on the type of sin. Through this system, God was teaching His people about His dual qualities of divine justice and mercy. God is just. He doesn't sweep sin under the rug or pretend it didn't happen. He's also merciful. He provides a way for us to be spared from punishment for sin.

When Jesus arrived, John the Baptist proclaimed Him to be "the Lamb of God, who takes away the sin of the world" (John 1:29). The title "Lamb of God" reminds us of Jesus' passive obedience. Isaiah 53, written seven hundred years before Christ was born, says, "Like a lamb that is led to the slaughter, and like a sheep that before its shearers is silent, so He opened not His mouth" (v. 7). Jesus allowed Himself to be killed. He didn't resist. He permitted it, becoming the final sacrifice for sin. We deserve the death He suffered, but in His great mercy, He became our substitute.

Jesus' active and passive obedience come together in Philippians 2:7–8. The passage describes Jesus "taking the form of a servant" (active obedience) and "becoming obedient to the point of death, even death on a cross" (passive obedience). Jesus was perfectly obedient to His Father's will. And He submitted Himself to death. "It is finished."

The greatest life ever lived had come to an end. The payment for sin had been made.

It was finished.

Ongoing Grace

The Greek word for "It is finished"—*tetelestai*—is in the perfect tense in Greek. That's significant because the perfect tense conveys an action that was completed in the past with results continuing into the present. It's different from the past tense, which looks back to an event and says, "This happened." The perfect tense adds the idea that this happened and is still in effect today. When Jesus cried out, "It is finished," He was saying, "It was finished in the past, it is still finished in the present, and it will remain finished in the future."

Let me ask you a question: Does your life reflect that Christ's work is finished? Or is your soul resisting Christ's grace, as if more work still is needed? Do you live under an unrelenting burden of guilt? Do you apply tremendous pressure to yourself, as if God were judging you based on your performance, not Christ's? If you struggle in these areas—as many of us do—our Savior has three words for you:

It is finished.

Jesus' work on the cross could not be any more finished than it is right now! His sacrifice was more than sufficient to atone for every sin you've committed, even the ones that haunt you. Those sins, too, are washed away by your Savior's blood. Jesus' death has earned for you complete acceptance in God's eyes. *His* performance has met the Father's approval. You and I cannot add to Jesus' work. We don't need to. He did it all for us.

Jesus' words from the cross communicate God's ongoing commitment to you and me. The payment for our sins happened in full. It doesn't wear off. It doesn't expire. You can't cancel it out. Jesus' sacrifice stands for all time. Therefore, God is eternally committed to you. He will be your rock and refuge in every instance without exception.

Jesus did not quit on the cross. He finished His work. He doesn't quit on you. He doesn't give up on you. He continues to support you by His grace so that you may be a person of grace to others.

From beginning to end, you are His. What He starts, He finishes. "He who began a good work in you will bring it to completion at the day of Jesus Christ" (Philippians 1:6).

Discussion Questions

1. What does Jesus' sixth statement from the cross teach us about our Savior?

2. Describe a time when you wanted to quit something. What made you want to quit? What was the outcome?

3. When is it a good idea to quit something? How do you know when it's best to quit?

4. Tell about a project you carried through to completion. What kept you going?

5. Read Romans 5:3–5. What does the passage teach about the value of perseverance?

6. Galatians 6:9 promises a harvest "if we do not give up." Right now, in what area of life do you need to be encouraged not to give up?

7. What does it mean to you that Jesus finished His work of salvation?

8. Based on what you read in this chapter, how can you be a person of grace this week?

It was now about the sixth hour, and there was darkness over the whole land until the ninth hour, while the sun's light failed. And the curtain of the temple was torn in two. Then Jesus, calling out with a loud voice, said, **"Father, into Your hands I commit My spirit!"** *And having said this He breathed His last.*

LUKE 23:44–46

CHAPTER 11

INTO YOUR HANDS

Take a moment to look at your hands. Observe them carefully. What do you see?

You may see smooth, moisturized hands. Or dry hands after washing a tall stack of dishes. Or rough hands from working out in the shop. You may see callouses from lifting weights, swinging a baseball bat, or playing guitar. You may see long, skinny fingers or short, stubby fingers. You might see a wedding ring or a class ring or a ring inherited from a family member. You might see a scar or a crooked finger. Everyone's hands tell a unique story.

Hands can do many good things. Hands deliver babies, bathe infants, and change diapers. A firm handshake or embrace welcomes. With our hands, we prepare and serve meals. We salute the flag or place our hand over our heart. Hands cover a cut with a bandage, and highly skilled hands perform surgery. Hands create beauty—painting, sculpting, woodworking. The deaf "hear" through sign language. We affirm with clapping or by writing a thank-you note.

Of course, in our broken world, hands have a dark side too. Human hands are responsible for pain. Hands hang up on someone or slam the door in a person's face. Hands communicate displeasure with another driver. Hands type angry emails and vitriolic social media posts. While a person's lips may say one thing, a hand with crossed fingers says the opposite. Hands steal. Hands pull the trigger on innocent people.

The vilest act of all time was when hands assaulted and killed Jesus. Hands slapped Him. Hands cracked a whip against His skin. Hands pressed a crown of thorns on His head. Hands nailed Him to the cross. Pilate washed his hands to disassociate himself, but the Creed reminds us otherwise: "He suffered under Pontius Pilate, was crucified, died, and was buried." Peter preached on the first Christian Pentecost, "This Jesus, delivered up according to the definite plan and foreknowledge of God, you crucified and killed by the *hands* of lawless men" (Acts 2:23, emphasis added).

God's Hands

Jesus' sixth statement from the cross was "It is finished." Mission accomplished. Jesus fulfilled the prophecies. He lived the perfect life, the only acceptable sacrifice for our guilty hands.

Once it was finished, Jesus spoke a final time: "Father, into Your hands I commit My spirit" (Luke 23:46). Then He breathed His last. Jesus committed Himself into His Father's hands.

God's hands are radically different from ours. While "God is spirit" (John 4:24) and doesn't literally have hands, in Jewish thought and language, the hand signaled strength or power. God's hands represented His sovereign power.

God has power to create: "O LORD, You are our Father; we are the clay, and You are our potter; we are all the work of Your hand" (Isaiah 64:8).

God has power to deliver: "It is because the LORD loves you and is keeping the oath that He swore to your fathers, that the LORD has brought you out with a mighty hand and redeemed you from the house of slavery, from the hand of Pharaoh king of Egypt" (Deuteronomy 7:8).

Human hands may exercise some power, but God's hands are supreme. At the end, Jesus committed His spirit into His Father's hands.

The Spirit Departs

Jesus' final words from the cross acknowledged what happens when a person dies: the spirit departs.

Every human being has two parts, the material and the spiritual. You are body and soul. Death, as an intrusion to God's good creation, rips apart the two elements of our being. When a believer dies, the body remains, and the spirit goes to be with the Lord.

Sometimes people will say they're ready for that moment of separation between body and soul. Older folks especially may say that their bodies are worn out and they're looking forward to departing this life. However, despite their readiness, *we're* often not ready to release our loved ones.

I spoke with a church member the other day after her stepfather died. The family wasn't certain about his faith. The stepdaughter told me that she and other family members talked to him repeatedly about Jesus at the end. They wanted to ensure that when it was time, he was ready.

We can prepare extensively. We can finalize wills and other documents. We can make advance arrangements with a funeral home. We can determine who gets which belongings. We can write letters to loved ones expressing our final thoughts. We can do all these things, but the only way to be completely ready is to be at peace with God through faith in Jesus.

By faith in Jesus, you're ready. At your last hour, when it's time for your spirit to depart, you can look to Him and know that by His grace, you're prepared to exit this life.

Jesus was ready. In His final words from the cross, Jesus committed His spirit to His heavenly Father, and then our Savior breathed His last.

Gracefully Letting Go

As the master of grace under pressure, Jesus was fully in control of Himself and the situation. The author of life had to give death permission. Previously Jesus had said, "For this reason the Father loves Me, because I lay down My life that I may take it up again. No one takes it from Me, but I lay it down of My own accord" (John 10:17–18). Life didn't escape from Jesus' body. He released Himself. Of His own initiative, Jesus breathed His last.

Interestingly, in the narratives of Jesus' crucifixion, none of the four Gospels say that He died. Matthew says Jesus "yielded up His spirit" (27:50). Mark and Luke say Jesus "breathed His last" (Mark 15:37; Luke 23:46). John says Jesus "bowed His head and gave up His spirit" (19:30).

None of the Gospel writers suggest that death took Jesus. In all four accounts, Jesus is active in His final moment, not passive. Death didn't snatch Him away. He yielded His spirit. He breathed His last. He gave up His spirit.

The Gospel writers were convinced of Jesus' authority to lay down His life and to take it up again.

Trusting God

Jesus' final words from the cross were a proclamation of trust. His seventh and final statement echoed Scripture, just as His fourth statement quoted Psalm 22. Psalm 31:5 says, "Into Your hand I commit my spirit; You have redeemed me, O LORD, faithful God." Jewish parents taught these words to their children as an evening prayer. A modern equivalent would be this prayer: "Now I lay me down to sleep. I pray the Lord my soul to keep. Thy love go with me through the night and wake me with the morning light." Another version of this prayer ends like so: "If I should die before I wake, I pray the Lord my soul to take." My wife and I pray the first version with our children every night, along with the Lord's Prayer.

When the sun sets each day, we're in the Lord's hands throughout the night. When our eyes close for the final time, we're in the Lord's hands throughout eternity.

"Into Your hands I commit My spirit." These are words of trust. Words of peace with God. Words of hopeful expectation. Words of faith.

Several people throughout history have imitated our Savior in His last words. Jesus' last words reportedly were the last words of many famous people, including the emperor Charlemagne, Christopher Columbus, and Martin Luther.

What a marked contrast to other famous last words.

Some die with a keen awareness of life slipping away. Frank Sinatra's last words: "I'm losing it."

Some die with a distorted feeling of failure. Leonardo da Vinci's last words: "I have offended God and mankind because my work did not reach the quality it should have."

Some die realizing how hard life has become. Benjamin Franklin's last words: "A dying man can do nothing easy."

Some die unimpressed by life. Winston Churchill's final words: "I'm bored with it all."[26]

And then there are Jesus' last words: "Into Your hands I commit My spirit."

Gracefully Living while Dying

A decade ago, my dear friend Jim modeled graceful living while he was dying. Every Wednesday, before heading to work, Jim would attend my weekly Bible study. One day, he told me grim news: He had been diagnosed with prostate cancer. Privately before the class started, he asked for permission to tell the group. He then stood before his friends and shared. He spoke with courage and expressed firm confidence that the Lord would sustain him in his battle.

Jim, a type-A engineer, pictured God as the ultimate planner. Jim didn't understand why he had cancer, just as none of us fully understand why bad things happen. Yet in the mystery, Jim trusted God. He said to me on many occasions, "It's all part of God's plan." Because of the cross, Jim knew that God loved him, and that was enough for him.

I had the privilege of driving Jim to his final doctor's appointment. It was one of the great honors of my ministry. We chatted in the car and then in the waiting room for a while. We talked about his parents and his upbringing. We talked about life. His perspective never wavered. God had a plan. He had a plan for Jim's life from beginning to end and into eternity. Because of Jesus, Jim believed what the apostle Paul wrote:

> **So we do not lose heart. Though our outer self is wasting away, our inner self is being renewed day by day. For this light momentary affliction is preparing for us an eternal weight of glory beyond all comparison. (2 Corinthians 4:16–17)**

For Jim's funeral, the church was packed like a Christmas Eve service. At the reception, sons Chris and Michael spoke about their dad. They exuded peace about where their dad was—no longer with them, but now in the arms of Jesus.

In the years after Jim's death, his wife, Khristi, continued her faithful involvement at church. When asked how she was doing, she was honest about the hard days. She'd post on social media about activities she and Jim used to do together, like yard work. She was sad—appropriately so—but not in despair. Her faith in Christ led her onward. Recently, Khristi relocated to be closer to her mom to help her as needed, choosing a new purpose for her new season in life.

God's sustaining grace upheld Jim and his family throughout those difficult years of living while dying. As a family, they walked through the valley of the shadow of death, holding the hand of their Savior. They exhibited courage. They lived with hope that God had a plan, and His plan culminated in eternal life.

Easter Hope

Because Jesus lives, we will live. Jesus' final words from the cross point ahead to His resurrection. His sixth word looked backward on His completed work. "It is finished." His seventh word looked ahead to a reunion with His heavenly Father. Payment for sin was accomplished. Glory awaited with the Father.

With Easter in mind, Lutheran commentator R. C. H. Lenski suggests translating a different word than "commit" or "entrust" in Jesus' final statement. Lenski prefers "deposit," writing in his commentary on Luke's Gospel, "We misunderstand when we see here complete submission, a placing in God's hands so that He may do as He desires with the spirit of Jesus; no, this is a committing only for the space of three days. Jesus lays down His life and He takes it up again (John 10:17–18)."[27]

Lenski is right. Jesus promised that He would lay down His life to take it up again! When He committed His spirit to the Father, it was a temporary deposit. More was coming. His rest in the tomb was an interlude in His earthly ministry. He rose from the tomb on the third day, emerging with the gift of life for all who believe!

Because of the cross and the empty tomb, we are in the Lord's hands forever. Not just for a season. Not just when we feel strong in our faith. Forever!

Read again the full verse from Psalm 31:5: "Into Your hand I commit my spirit; You have redeemed me, O LORD, faithful God." Jesus died to redeem us, to rescue us from the eternal consequences of sin, from the finality of death, and from the grasp of the devil.

Death is defeated. By dying on the cross, Jesus conquered death, ensuring for us unending life. For that reason, we declare, "Death is swallowed up in victory. O death, where is your victory? O death, where is your sting?" (1 Corinthians 15:54–55).

At the end, Jesus entrusted His life to the Father. At our end, we, too, can entrust our lives to the Father. Jesus' cross is our assurance, and His empty tomb is our confidence.

Daily, we commit our spirits to our heavenly Father, trusting Him. As Jesus said in John 10:28, "I give them eternal life, and they will never perish, and no one will snatch them out of My hand."

Pierced Hands

Everyone's hands tell a story. Jesus' hands tell the greatest story of all. The nail marks tell the story of God's love for us. The holes prove God's determination to restore us to Him. The holes forever testify to Jesus' love for us, as God says in Isaiah 49:16: "Behold, I have engraved you on the palms of My hands."

For Jesus, these words were true literally. On Easter evening, Jesus appeared to His disciples. The following Sunday, He appeared to them again. This time Thomas was with them. He had been absent when Jesus first visited.

Thomas wanted proof, and he specified what type of proof he expected. He wanted to see the marks. Not the marks of thorns pressed into Jesus' head. Not the marks of flagellation on Jesus' back. Not even the marks of nails through Jesus' feet. Thomas wanted to see His hands.

Jesus presented the evidence. Thomas saw. He touched. And he believed, exclaiming, "My Lord and my God!" (John 20:28).

It has been suggested that at the resurrection of all flesh on the Last Day, all scars will be gone with one exception. By God's grace, you and I will have perfect bodies. Not one blemish or defect. Not one scar.

But Jesus' scars will remain. In His resurrected body, He retained the nail marks. They're an eternal reminder of all that He did to redeem you. His scars remain as an everlasting statement that He died for you, and now your life is committed into His strong hands.

Discussion Questions

1. What does Jesus' seventh statement from the cross teach us about our Savior?

2. Isaiah 64:8 declares that we are the work of God's hand. How does that affect your view of yourself?

3. Have you ever heard someone who, nearing the end of life, said she or he was ready to die? What made that person feel ready?

4. Were you taught any bedtime prayers as a child? Share with the group.

5. The last words of several famous people were listed in the chapter. Did any of the parting words strike you? Explain why.

6. How does Easter shape your view of the cross? of death?

7. What things are out of your hands but in the Lord's? How can that knowledge provide comfort?

8. Based on what you read in this chapter, how can you be a person of grace this week?

But we have this treasure in jars of clay, to show that the surpassing power belongs to God and not to us. We are afflicted in every way, but not crushed; perplexed, but not driven to despair; persecuted, but not forsaken; struck down, but not destroyed; always carrying in the body the death of Jesus, so that the life of Jesus may also be manifested in our bodies. For we who live are always being given over to death for Jesus' sake, so that the life of Jesus also may be manifested in our mortal flesh.

2 CORINTHIANS 4:7–11

GOD'S TOOLS FOR GRACEFUL LIVING

Throughout the ages, believers have combatted stress through their faith. Scripture points us to "our refuge and strength" in every time of need: the Lord Almighty (Psalm 46:1). In His provision for us, God lovingly places into our hands tools for responding to stress gracefully. Specifically, God's Word points us to prayer, Scripture, and a God-shaped perspective.

Prayer

The psalmists understood stress. The word *distress* appears twenty times in the Book of Psalms, more than double its occurrences in any other book. But with God, there's always hope! Many instances of distress in the Psalms are paired with divine promises.

- In my distress I called upon the LORD; to my God I cried for help. From His temple He heard my voice, and my cry to Him reached His ears. (Psalm 18:6)

- But I will sing of Your strength; I will sing aloud of Your steadfast love in the morning. For You have been to me a fortress and a refuge in the day of my distress. (Psalm 59:16)

* Then they cried to the LORD in their trouble, and He delivered them from their distress. (Psalm 107:6, 13, 19, 28)

* Out of my distress I called on the LORD; the LORD answered me and set me free. (Psalm 118:5)

The psalmists discovered a predictable pattern: They called out in distress, and God responded. Should we expect any less? God hears our voices. He is our deliverer, and He is listening.

How does stress move you? Does it move you to complain to others? Does it move you to lash out in frustration? Or does it move you to prayer?

In the summer of 2020, my congregation hosted a prayer vigil. We called it "Speak Up: A Prayer Vigil for Healing and Peace in America." We met for one hour and, using the Lord's Prayer as an outline, prayed about a variety of difficult issues, including rising COVID-19 cases and racial unrest. We devoted considerable time to silence so that people could present specific burdens to the Lord. For days afterward, church members remarked how an hour of prayer refreshed their souls and helped them cope with stress.

Prayer comforted the souls of the psalmists. Prayer comforts the souls of saints today. By God's grace, praying in stressful times can soothe your soul too. And with your soul comforted, you're better equipped to respond to stress gracefully.

Scripture

Another stress reliever that God's Word presents is . . . God's Word! In Psalm 119:143, the writer declares, "Trouble and anguish have found me out, but Your commandments are my delight." The New Living Translation begins the verse, "As pressure and stress bear down on me." Isn't that what it feels like? Stress bears down on us. It's an oppressive weight.

The second half of the verse reveals the psalmist's strength: "But Your commandments are my delight." In Psalm 119, the psalmist uses a variety of synonyms for Scripture, words like *commandments, rules, testimonies, words, promise, precepts, law,* and *statutes.* The psalmist delights in God's Word. In stressful times, we can delight in God's Word.

Consider everything that goes into your mind. Disastrous events dominate TV newscasts and online news feeds. You may hear negative comments from people around you. Our minds can be flooded with news and words that drag us down.

What if you tipped the balance more toward God's Word? What if more of your mental input came from the Bible and less from the world? Philippians 4:8 says, "Finally, brothers, whatever is true, whatever is honorable, whatever is just, whatever is pure, whatever is lovely, whatever is commendable, if there is any excellence, if there is anything worthy of praise, think about these things." The following verse promises that "the God of peace will be with you" (Philippians 4:9).

If you want more stress, fill your mind with stressful words—the latest crime report, the political banter, anything negative and unnerving. Or you can choose the alternative: combat stress with God's life-giving Word. Our emotional capacity is limited. Therefore, seek fewer toxic influences and more uplifting content.

God's Word shapes our thoughts and actions. "Your Word is a lamp to my feet and a light to my path" (Psalm 119:105). God's Word leads us in a more graceful path. His Word teaches us His ways. Through His life-giving Word, He liberates us from an onslaught of negativity and frees us to live more optimistically and joyfully.

Godly Perspective

One of the most vivid New Testament passages about stress is in 2 Corinthians 4, known as the "jars of clay" passage. Paul described believers as fragile clay vessels filled with a great treasure!

Paul knew about fragility. Two chapters later, he listed his resumé of trials. Talk about stressful! Beatings, imprisonments, riots, sleeplessness, hunger, sorrow. The apostle was just getting warmed up. He goes into greater detail in chapter 11. Imprisoned, flogged, stoned, shipwrecked, cold, naked, concerned about the churches. He shouldered major stress.

But he persevered. The apostle testified, "We are afflicted in every way, but not crushed; perplexed, but not driven to despair; persecuted, but not forsaken; struck down, but not destroyed" (2 Corinthians 4:8–9). The New International Version translates the first part as "hard pressed on every side, but not crushed." Hard pressed. We feel pressure. But we're not crushed!

In Christ, we're not crushed. Do you know why? Because Christ fills us! We're not empty vessels. We are "always carrying in the body the death of Jesus, so that the life of Jesus may also be manifested in our bodies" (v. 10). If you're a believer, you're *always* carrying Jesus within you. A vessel filled with a firm substance can be cracked but not crushed—and nothing is more solid than the Savior!

A godly perspective sustained Paul in his severe trials. In the midst of hardships, he knew that God was with him. Paul believed that God would not forsake him. Paul trusted that God would accomplish the purposes He intended, no matter how bleak the situation.

None of us would choose hardship for ourselves. The positive by-product of challenges is that once we've endured them, we see how God's sustaining grace carried us. Personal experience convinces us of God's faithfulness. As Paul wrote in what is presumed to be his final letter, "The Lord will rescue me from every evil deed and bring me safely into His heavenly kingdom" (2 Timothy 4:18). Paul responded to his trials confidently because God had brought him through previous adversity.

God will guide us through stressful times. With that assurance, we can approach challenges with greater calm and composure.

By His grace, the Lord equips us with faith-building tools for combatting stress: prayer, Scripture, and a God-shaped perspective. The pressures of life may be unrelenting, but so is the love of God for you! Even if you look back with disappointment on previous defeats in the battle against stress, today is a new day! With the Lord's help, you can respond to challenges more gracefully today than you did yesterday. His sustaining grace makes it possible!

Discussion Questions

1. Has prayer helped you through a stressful time? If so, share how prayer helped.

2. What kinds of things have you put into your mind today? How have those things affected your mood and outlook?

3. Psalm 119:105 says, "Your Word is a lamp to my feet and a light to my path." Think of a time when something you read in the Bible guided you in a decision or action.

4. How does faith in Christ give us a different perspective on life's hardships?

5. When have you been most aware of your fragility?

6. To you, what does it mean to be "hard pressed on every side, but not crushed" (2 Corinthians 4:8 NIV)?

7. Share three takeaways from this book.

8. Complete the sentence: Beginning today, with God's help, I will be a more graceful person by . . .

LEADER GUIDE

The saying is true: There's strength in numbers. It's not just a matter of practical insight but also a biblical truth. "Two are better than one, because they have a good reward for their toil. For if they fall, one will lift up his fellow. But woe to him who is alone when he falls and has not another to lift him up!" (Ecclesiastes 4:9–10).

The following pages are a guide to assist you in facilitating group discussion. Encourage participants to write answers in the book before you meet as a group so that everyone has thoughtfully prepared for the discussion time. During group discussion, take your time. It's better to dwell on a question that generates good conversation than to rush through the material. You might prioritize questions ahead of time in case you need to skip some.

God bless you as you take hold of the truth expressed in His Word!

Chapter 1: Living Gracefully

1. **Complete this sentence from your own observations or experiences: Ungraceful behavior is . . .**

   Define what the book means by the term *ungraceful*. Encourage participants to reflect on their own instances of ungracefulness. This reflection will help them see their need for the material in the book.

2. **Now complete this sentence: We live gracefully when . . .**

   Define what the book means when it uses the term *graceful*. In humility, direct participants to think of others who have acted gracefully. This reflection will help paint a picture of a desired future.

3. **How can a person be graceful and still be raw and honest about his or her struggles?**

   Help group members to think in terms of both/and. We can be graceful and still be raw and honest. We don't have to project a perfect life to appear graceful.

4. **Choose one of the character studies referenced: David, Daniel, Esther, or Stephen. Read that person's story, as listed in the chapter. Discuss how that story demonstrates graceful behavior.**

   For the sake of time, you might assign this activity as homework and debrief before the next session. Be intentional about relating the Bible story to the lessons of graceful living from the chapter.

5. **Why do we need the Holy Spirit's help to live gracefully? What does He do that we can't do for ourselves?**

   This question acknowledges our sinful inability to live gracefully as we should. Consider the identity and function of the Holy Spirit. The section on the Third Article of the Creed in the Small Catechism is a helpful resource on the doctrine of the Holy Spirit.

6. **Review the fruit of the Spirit in Galatians 5:22–23. Which of the fruit do you most desire for yourself right now?**

   Ask participants to elaborate on why they chose a specific fruit. Stretch their thinking by asking them to imagine what types of behaviors would demonstrate that fruit manifesting itself.

7. **If you were to live more gracefully, what effect might that have on the people around you?**

   Remind group members that we live not for ourselves but for Jesus, who calls us to love Him and love our neighbor as ourselves (Matthew 22:37–39). When we live more gracefully, that benefits not only us but also the people around us, especially those closest to us.

8. **What do you hope to gain from reading this book?**

   Encourage participants to share aloud and also write down their answer to this question. At the end of the book, they can look back and see how their expectations match up with their actual experience with the book.

Chapter 2: God's Perspective on Stress

1. Stress has been called a national epidemic. Do you feel that claim is accurate or an overstatement? Explain your answer.

    Encourage specific examples of where people see stress in society.

2. Do you ever sense other people's stress around you? Share an example, if possible.

    Ask participants if they can perceive tension within other people and if that tension seems to be increasing.

3. In the chapter, several statistics are cited as evidence of societal distress. Which of the statistics can you relate to most?

    Participants may choose one of the statistics and share how they see it manifested in real life.

4. Do you thrive under deadlines? Or does last-minute work stress you out? How might you deal with someone who's the opposite of you in this department?

    Listen as each person shares how he or she reacts to deadline pressure. Notice how God has wired people differently. Welcome suggestions on how to relate to people who are opposites.

5. What causes you more stress: your own foolishness, personal circumstances beyond your control, or godlessness around you? Explain your answer.

    This question may require extra thought as participants weigh the three options.

6. **How do you cope when the cause of stress is outside your control?**

    Listen for practical insights. Either through research before the meeting or through responses to this question, you might compile a list of tips that can be shared with the group afterward.

7. **It has been said that good leaders keep their heads when everyone else is losing theirs. How might you keep your head when others are stressed?**

    This question ties into the main theme of grace under pressure. The goal of the study is to continually keep the theme of grace in front of participants as they consider stressful situations.

8. **How can the group pray for you in the stresses you may be facing currently?**

    Allow everyone to share. Keep notes of their needs. Pray for them today, and next week follow up by asking about the areas of stress each person identified. You might also have everyone in the group pair up as prayer partner who pray for each other specifically throughout the week.

Chapter 3: Did Jesus Ever Crack under Pressure?

1. **How do you view Jesus' actions in cleansing the temple? Do you find His behavior shocking or out of character? Explain.**

   For many people, Jesus' actions in the temple are surprising. Some who are familiar with the story may not feel as shocked by it. Challenge participants to imagine this is the first time they've encountered the story.

2. **Jesus felt stress but never sinned. Ephesians 4:26 says, "Be angry and do not sin." What does that verse mean to you?**

   Help participants to understand that anger in itself is a feeling, not a sin. What we do with our anger can be either God-pleasing or sinful.

3. **Think of someone who would benefit from you becoming more patient. If you're comfortable sharing, tell the group and ask them to hold you accountable.**

   This question allows participants to reflect on relationships in which they have a short fuse. Through commitment and accountability, your group members can cultivate greater patience.

4. **How do you deal with criticism directed at you? Think of how you might be able to handle criticism better.**

   This is another question aimed at self-improvement with the Holy Spirit's help. To establish a common definition, you might explore the difference between suggestions and criticism.

5. **Do you feel stress because of expectations? Where do the expectations come from?**

    Many times we place demanding expectations on ourselves that may or may not be appropriate. Help participants to identify the root of heavy expectations.

6. **Have you been in physical danger before? Share with the group.**

    Be prepared for personal stories that could become emotional.

7. **Share one practical insight you gained from the chapter and how you plan to apply it in the week ahead.**

    Help participants to think through how to apply the truths of the chapter in concrete ways.

8. **From previous experience, what has helped you to handle stress well?**

    This question allows participants to share a win, an occasion when they responded to stress well. Celebrating previous successes can instill confidence—"With God's help, I *can* respond well to stress!" Participants can also share helpful tools and strategies with others.

Chapter 4: Unparalleled Pressure: The Cross

1. **Share anything new you learned about crucifixion from the chapter.**

    Insights could be a brand-new fact or simply thinking about a previously known fact in a new way.

2. **Why do you think crucifixion was the capital punishment of choice for the Roman government?**

    Consider the effect of crucifixion on its victims and witnesses, along with what the Romans hoped to achieve through such a torturous death.

3. **Do you think the cross has been "tamed" in today's society by its use as art and decor?**

    Name examples of the cross in art and decor. Evaluate how well those examples convey the true nature of the cross.

4. **Describe the worst physical pain you've experienced. What did you say to yourself in the midst of the pain?**

    Be prepared for emotional answers as participants recall past experiences. This question reinforces Jesus' love for us—that He chose to be in pain to save us.

5. **What do you think motivated the onlookers to verbally abuse Jesus?**

    Consider why people say hurtful things. Take into account how the onlookers might have felt about Jesus.

6. In today's culture, with social media and other platforms, do you feel that verbal abuse is on the rise? Explain your answer.

    This question invites participants to explore the impact of modern technologies on how we communicate with one another through spoken, written, and typed words.

7. In the cross, we see the dehumanizing effect of public humiliation. What kinds of truths might help someone who has been humiliated or embarrassed to rebuild his or her self-image?

    Think of positive messages that could bring healing to a person who has been torn down.

8. Considering what you read in the chapter, how does it feel to know that Jesus suffered and died on the cross for you?

    This question reminds participants that everything Jesus endured was to save them from their sins.

Chapter 5: Father, Forgive Them

1. **What does Jesus' first statement from the cross teach us about our Savior?**

   Reflect on what Jesus' words reveal about His nature, character, values, and purpose.

2. **How does ignorance lead to sin?**

   Define *ignorance*. Consider the connection between lack of understanding and sinful words, thoughts, actions, and inaction.

3. **Should people be considered responsible for sins committed in ignorance? Why or why not?**

   This question explores the extent of personal responsibility—whether "I didn't know any better" is a valid excuse. Consider concrete examples of people acting in ignorance, such as children who haven't learned a certain behavior concept yet, an employee who wasn't told expectations clearly, or an immigrant who didn't understand the laws of the land. Discuss times when people acting in ignorance should be "let off the hook" versus when they should be held accountable.

4. **Tell about a time you interceded or advocated for someone else. How about a time when you did this for someone who sinned against you?**

   Allow participants a moment to think of a time when they stood up for someone else and share as they are willing.

5. The chapter made a distinction between forgiveness and reconciliation. How can we feel at peace if we're not completely reconciled with another person?

Consider what peace is really all about. Connect peace to our relationship to God through Jesus, a constant reality regardless of what may or may not happen in our lives.

6. What does it look like to overcome evil with good?

Encourage specific examples of people responding to evil with good actions. Process how a grace-filled response can change the nature of a situation.

7. How can your small group intercede in prayer for you this week?

Note prayer requests. You can consult your notes during the week or at the next Bible study meeting for follow-up. If you arranged for prayer partners, you might check in to see how the partnering is going.

8. Based on what you read in this chapter, how can you be a person of grace this week?

Encourage participants to apply Jesus' words from the cross to their own efforts to live gracefully as His ambassadors.

Chapter 6: You Will Be with Me in Paradise

1. **What does Jesus' second statement from the cross teach us about our Savior?**

   Reflect on what Jesus' words reveal about His nature, character, values, and purpose.

2. **What comfort do you find in the story of the redeemed thief?**

   Reflect on the message of grace and forgiveness the story provides.

3. **What does the story teach us about the nature of God's grace?**

   Discuss what God's grace is and is not. Talk about what God's grace does in the lives of people.

4. **Have you ever struggled with the concept of life being unfair? Please share.**

   Answers could range from minor annoyances to significant heartache. Be prepared for the possibility of emotional answers.

5. **Tell about a time when you received better than you deserved.**

   This question invites gratitude. Everything we have is a gift from God.

6. **How can you give others better than they deserve?**

   Encourage participants to think of instances when a person might do something normally deemed unworthy of a kind response. Imagine a response based on grace.

7. **Whose conversion can you pray for?**

    Make a list of unbelievers (pre-Christians!). As a group, commit to praying for them by name during the week. Pray for the Holy Spirit to touch their hearts and lead them to faith in the only Savior, Jesus.

8. **Based on what you read in this chapter, how can you be a person of grace this week?**

    Encourage participants to apply Jesus' words from the cross to their own efforts to live gracefully as His ambassadors.

Chapter 7: Behold, Your Son; Behold, Your Mother

1. **What does Jesus' third statement from the cross teach us about our Savior?**

    Reflect on what Jesus' words reveal about His nature, character, values, and purpose.

2. **Use your imagination for a fun question. If Me Church really existed, what do you hope it would offer?**

    This is a lighthearted question designed to generate laughs and build community. If necessary, steer discussion away from complaints or gripes, and encourage participants to respond gracefully.

3. **What helps you to forget about yourself for a moment and attend to others' needs?**

    Encourage participants to think of times when they were absorbed in others' needs and lost sight of their own troubles for a while.

4. **What do you make of the fact that Mary was *standing* at the cross? In this regard, how is she an example to us?**

    Explore what Mary's standing posture says about her resolve in the face of tragedy. Consider how her faith gave her such extraordinary strength at the cross.

5. **Why do you think John was the only disciple at the cross? What did he have to overcome personally to be there?**

    Review the events of Jesus' arrest and trial, as all the disciples forsook Him. Put yourself in John's shoes. Imagine his grief and the courage it took to return to Jesus at the cross.

6. **Mary and John both experienced intense grief over the loss of a son and best friend. What has helped you to deal with grief?**

    Be prepared for emotional responses as feelings of grief may resurface. Be a comforting, compassionate presence for those still deeply affected by loss. Grief can be over the death of loved ones or other losses in life—loss of health, a job, or the like.

7. **The chapter lists pairings of believers who supported one another. Besides a spouse, tell about someone God has given you for mutual encouragement.**

    Celebrate God's gift of companionship for the sometimes-bumpy journey of life.

8. **Based on what you read in this chapter, how can you be a person of grace this week?**

    Encourage participants to apply Jesus' words from the cross to their own efforts to live gracefully as His ambassadors.

Chapter 8: Why Have You Forsaken Me?

1. **What does Jesus' fourth statement from the cross teach us about our Savior?**

    Reflect on what Jesus' words reveal about His nature, character, values, and purpose.

2. **Are "Why, Lord?" questions productive? Why or why not?**

    It might help to use a specific example when a "Why, Lord?" question might be asked. Remind participants that it's not wrong to ask "Why, Lord?" After all, Jesus asked the question.

3. **The chapter presents three theories about Jesus' question from the cross. Which of the theories resonates with you most?**

    Guide participants in weighing the pros and cons of each theory.

4. **If you were present that day, what might you have interpreted Jesus' fourth statement to mean?**

    Remind participants that onlookers didn't have the Gospels or Epistles, as we do, to explain the significance of the cross. Help them to imagine themselves watching Jesus' death in real time and hearing His words as He spoke them.

5.   What is your reaction to Mother Teresa's "dark letters"? How do her struggles compare with your struggles?

Review what participants know about Mother Teresa. You might want to research her beforehand and even read an article about her "dark letters." Many people are surprised to learn that such a highly esteemed Christian leader experienced deep valleys in her faith.

6.   Read Psalm 22. What words or phrases stand out to you? How does it remind you of Jesus? Do any words or phrases connect to your life experiences?

Encourage participants to underline, highlight, or write impactful words and phrases.

7.   What difference does it make in your life to know that God will never forsake you?

Help participants to envision circumstances when God's promise of fidelity would provide the greatest comfort.

8.   Based on what you read in this chapter, how can you be a person of grace this week?

Encourage participants to apply Jesus' words from the cross to their own efforts to live gracefully as His ambassadors.

Chapter 9: I Thirst

1. **What does Jesus' fifth statement from the cross teach us about our Savior?**

   Reflect on what Jesus' words reveal about His nature, character, values, and purpose.

2. **When you need to rehydrate, what's your preferred drink?**

   This question is designed to help the group get better acquainted as friends.

3. **From your own experience, what are signs of spiritual dehydration?**

   Answers may vary. God has wired all of us to respond differently in different circumstances. Common signs might include overly angry reactions, excessive worry, defensiveness, and lack of care for others.

4. **On a scale of 1 to 10, how spiritually hydrated are you right now? Explain your answer.**

   This question invites participants to examine their faith practices and spiritual health.

5. **The Bible says Jesus is our high priest who sympathizes with us in our weakness (Hebrews 4:15). What does that statement mean to you personally?**

   Explore what sympathy is all about and how sympathy relates to Jesus' experience as fully God and fully man.

6. **How did you stay connected to your church or faith community during the COVID-19 pandemic?**
    Invite participants to share their recollections of a challenging season for all.

7. **How can you tell that you're staying spiritually hydrated? What attitudes or actions give evidence of spiritual health in your life?**
    Encourage participants to identify behaviors demonstrating they're filled with God's Word and following the lead of His Spirit. Galatians 5:22–23 lists the fruit of the Spirit: love, joy, peace, patience, kindness, goodness, faithfulness, gentleness, and self-control.

8. **Based on what you read in this chapter, how can you be a person of grace this week?**
    Encourage participants to apply Jesus' words from the cross to their own efforts to live gracefully as His ambassadors.

Chapter 10: It Is Finished

1. **What does Jesus' sixth statement from the cross teach us about our Savior?**

    Reflect on what Jesus' words reveal about His nature, character, values, and purpose.

2. **Describe a time when you wanted to quit something. What made you want to quit? What was the outcome?**

    Be prepared for feelings of frustration to resurface as participants relive memories of difficult moments.

3. **When is it a good idea to quit something? How do you know when it's best to quit?**

    Challenge participants to expand their idea of quitting—not always as an admission of defeat but sometimes as a necessary choice.

4. **Tell about a project you carried through to completion. What kept you going?**

    This question is an opening for participants to share victories and to analyze key factors in perseverance.

5. **Read Romans 5:3–5. What does the passage teach about the value of perseverance?**

    Guide participants to reflect on key words in the passage.

6. **Galatians 6:9 promises a harvest "if we do not give up." Right now, in what area of life do you need to be encouraged not to give up?**

    This question invites vulnerability. Affirm participants' honesty as they open up about current struggles. Encourage participants in their struggles by praying for them, either together in the meeting or throughout the week.

7. **What does it mean to you that Jesus finished His work of salvation?**

    Consider the opposite: What it would mean if His work were unfinished.

8. **Based on what you read in this chapter, how can you be a person of grace this week?**

    Encourage participants to apply Jesus' words from the cross to their own efforts to live gracefully as His ambassadors.

Chapter 11: Into Your Hands

1. **What does Jesus' seventh statement from the cross teach us about our Savior?**

   Reflect on what Jesus' words reveal about His nature, character, values, and purpose.

2. **Isaiah 64:8 declares that we are the work of God's hand. How does that affect your view of yourself?**

   Consider what it means to be created by God in love. Encourage participants to see themselves as God's handiwork and the object of His affection through Christ.

3. **Have you ever heard someone who, nearing the end of life, said she or he was ready to die? What made that person feel ready?**

   Be prepared for emotional responses as participants may remember someone close to them who died.

4. **Were you taught any bedtime prayers as a child? Share with the group.**

   Reflect on the teachings of faith contained within each bedtime prayer.

5. **The last words of several famous people were listed in the chapter. Did any of the parting words strike you? Explain why.**

   Ponder what the words revealed about the person's outlook on life and death.

6.   **How does Easter shape your view of the cross? of death?**

   Easter is about the resurrection of Jesus, His triumph over death. Without Easter, Jesus' crucifixion would have a completely different significance. Listen as participants share their reflections on the cross in light of the empty tomb.

7.   **What things are out of your hands but in the Lord's? How can that knowledge provide comfort?**

   Allow time for participants to share current frustrations. Be empathetic in your words and body language. In a way that doesn't minimize problems but conveys faith and hope, remind the group that every situation is in the Lord's hands.

8.   **Based on what you read in this chapter, how can you be a person of grace this week?**

   Encourage participants to apply Jesus' words from the cross to their own efforts to live gracefully as His ambassadors.

Conclusion: God's Tools for Graceful Living

1.   **Has prayer helped you through a stressful time? If so, share how prayer helped.**
     Encourage participants to share what they prayed for, to whatever extent they're comfortable sharing.

2.   **What kinds of things have you put into your mind today? How have those things affected your mood and outlook?**
     Participants might recall news shows, articles, or conversations. Encourage them to reflect on the impact of that mental input.

3.   **Psalm 119:105 says, "Your Word is a lamp to my feet and a light to my path." Think of a time when something you read in the Bible guided you in a decision or action.**
     Encourage specificity in sharing what passage they read and how it shaped their behaviors.

4.   **How does faith in Christ give us a different perspective on life's hardships?**
     By contrast, consider what a person's perspective on hardships might be without faith in Christ.

5.   **When have you been most aware of your fragility?**
     It requires a degree of courage to respond to this question openly. Thank participants for their vulnerability.

6.   **To you, what does it mean to be "hard pressed on every side, but not crushed" (2 Corinthians 4:8 NIV)?**
     Consider the difference between being hard pressed (facing trouble) and being crushed (total defeat).

7.   **Share three takeaways from this book.**
     You might give a quick overview or review of the chapters to prompt thinking and discussion.

8.   **Complete the sentence: Beginning today, with God's help, I will be a more graceful person by . . .**
     Encourage participants to commit to their statements by writing the response in the book.

ACKNOWLEDGMENTS

I was incredibly honored that one of my heroes, Paul Maier, graciously agreed to write the foreword. Thank you, Dr. Maier! Thank you to my initial reviewers who took the time to read the manuscript and provide excellent feedback for improving it: Alice Klement, Gary Larsen, Daniel Mueller, and Shirley Yoakum. Thank you to my family for your constant love and support. Ashley, when God gave me such a wonderful wife, it was one of His greatest acts of grace! Caleb, Ethan, Emma, and Zachary, you bring me so much joy every day. Dad, Mom, and Kelly, you've always championed me as a writer and cheered me on. Thank you to the talented team at Concordia Publishing House, especially those who worked with this manuscript, Laura Lane and Jamie Moldenhauer. To the wonderful people of Shepherd of the Hills Lutheran Church, School, and Child Care: it's a joy to grow in God's grace with you!

NOTES

1   Richard Swenson, *Margin: Restoring Emotional, Physical, Financial, and Time Reserves to Overloaded Lives* (Colorado Springs: The Navigators, 1992), 45

2   "What Is Stress?" The American Institute of Stress, https://www.stress.org/daily -life; *Stress in America: Paying with Our Health*, American Psychological Association, February 4, 2015, https://www.apa.org/news/press/releases/stress /2014/stress-report.pdf.

3   Maureen Connolly and Margot Slade, "The United States of Stress 2019," *Everyday Health*, October 23, 2018, https://www.everydayhealth.com/wellness/united-states -of-stress/.

4   *Luther's Works* 22:233, 234.

5   "Crucifixion," *Encyclopedia Britannica*, October 12, 2018, https://www.britannica .com/topic/crucifixion-capital-punishment.

6   Paul L. Maier, trans., *Josephus: The Essential Writings* (Grand Rapids, MI: Kregel Publications, 1988), 341.

7   Maier, *Josephus*, 347.

8   N. T. Wright, *The Day the Revolution Began: Reconsidering the Meaning of Jesus' Crucifixion* (San Francisco: HarperOne, 2006), 54.

9   Wright, *The Day the Revolution Began*, 59.

10 Simon Wiesenthal tells his story in his book *The Sunflower: On the Possibilities and Limits of Forgiveness* (New York: Knopf Doubleday Publishing Group, 1969).

11 "Pray for You," by Jaron Lowenstein and Joel Brentlinger, track 9 on Jaron and the Long Road to Love, *Getting Dressed in the Dark*, Jaronwood Records, 2010.

12 Fulton J. Sheen, *The Cries of Jesus from the Cross: A Fulton Sheen Anthology*, comp. Al Smith (Manchester, NH: Sophia Institute Press, 2018), 101.

13 "The Petersen House," National Park Service, April 18, 2018, https://www.nps.gov /foth/the-petersen-house.htm.

14 "meChurch | Igniter Media | Church Video," Igniter Media, July 31, 2006, https:// youtu.be/cGEmlPjgjVI.

15 Large Catechism IV 70–71.

16 Sheen, *The Cries of Jesus from the Cross*, 213.

17 See Mother Teresa, *Come Be My Light: The Private Writings of the Saint of Calcutta*, ed. Brian Kolodiejchuk (New York: Doubleday, 2007), 149–77.

18   Darren Rovell, *First in Thirst* (New York: Amacom, 2005), 7.

19   Amelia Lucas, "Gatorade Is a Super Bowl Icon, but at Stores, Sports Drinks Are Fighting for Growth," CNBC, February 2, 2020, https://www.cnbc.com/2020/02/02 /gatorade-and-powerade-try-to-adapt-as-sports-drinks-sales-decline.html.

20   Joe Kays and Arline Phillips-Han, *Explore* 8, no. 1 (Spring 2003, https://research.ufl .edu/publications/explore/v08n1/gatorade.html

21   Ron Word, "Dr. Robert Cade, 80: Gatorade Inventor," *Toronto Star*, November 27, 2007, https://www.thestar.com/news/2007/11/27/dr_robert_cade_80_gatorade_ inventor.html.

22   Jennie Cohen, "7 Things You May Not Know about the Sistine Chapel," *History*, November 1, 2012, https://www.history.com/news/7-things-you-may-not-know -about-the-sistine-chapel.

23   The biography of Michelangelo by his friend and student Ascanio Condivi has been translated in Charles Holroyd, *Michael Angelo Buonarroti* (New York: Charles Scribner's Sons, 1903), https://www.gutenberg.org/files/19332/19332-pdf.pdf. See pages 44–45 for this account.

24   Variations of this anonymous prayer have circulated for many years on the internet; see this post, for example: https://www.beliefnet.com/prayers/protestant/morning /morning-prayer.aspx.

25   Oswald Chambers, "It Is Finished! (November 21)," in *My Utmost for His Highest*, https://utmost.org/it-is-finished/.

26   All these "last words" are found in Chris Higgins, "64 People and Their Famous Last Words," *Mental Floss*, February 12, 2016, https://www.mentalfloss.com/article /58534/64-people-and-their-famous-last-words.

27   R. C. H. Lenski, *Interpretation of St. Mark's and St. Luke's Gospels* (Columbus, OH: Lutheran Book Concern, 1934), 724.

CREDITS